seasonal
SLOW
KNITTING

seasonal
SLOW
KNITTING

THOUGHTFUL PROJECTS
FOR A HANDMADE YEAR

Hannah Thiessen

photography by Katie Starks

Editor: Meredith A. Clark
Designer: Danielle Youngsmith
Production Manager: Kathleen Gaffney

Library of Congress Control Number: 2020931030

ISBN: 978-1-4197-4043-5
eISBN: 978-1-64700-021-9

Printed and bound in China
10 9 8 7 6 5 4 3

Abrams books are available at special discounts
when purchased in quantity for premiums and
promotions as well as fundraising or educational
use. Special editions can also be created to
specification. For details, contact specialsales@
abramsbooks.com or the address below.

Abrams® is a registered trademark of
Harry N. Abrams, Inc.

 ABRAMS
The Art of Books

195 Broadway
New York, NY 10007
abramsbooks.com

table of contents

introduction:
returning to slow knitting

In early 2015, I submitted the idea for my book *Slow Knitting* to Abrams. The proposal was my first: my first attempt to write a book, my first attempt to pitch an idea this large to a completely unknown entity. In my email, I included a mood board, a single essay, and some notes about what I wanted to write: the idea that other knitters—and other crafters—may have been having the same feelings I was. I loved my craft, but I felt overwhelmed by knitting's new wave, an onslaught of what was a must-knit, which yarns were must-haves, what the color or notion of the moment was. I was longing for a sense of place within a craft that had been mine since I was a child but that was feeling increasingly more alien as I got older.

I loved casting on new projects, but not the idea that I needed to make them quickly, or that I needed to become a handmade-gift factory. I channeled my passion for knitting into a career in marketing, and I was becoming fatigued from the need to constantly be making something that other knitters would admire and talk about, while simultaneously guiding companies toward how to sell and share their products. The funny thing about knitting is that it feels inauthentic amid the messaging of constant sales. The idea that you have to buy more yarn, buy more patterns, and churn things out is incongruent with what knitting is: a peaceful moment to yourself, time away from the busyness of the world we live in, a celebration of material and patience. To me, this craft is authenticity and simplicity at their finest.

After the book was published in 2017, I discovered that much of my own knitting practice needed to change if I was going to match the values I had put forth in *Slow Knitting*. My stash seemed full to bursting, so I pulled anything and everything I wasn't madly in love with and sold it. I began slowing down my buying of patterns and more carefully selecting not just yarn but clothing, food, and items for my day-to-day life. It seemed disingenuous to go speak to how we should support small business, small farmers, and slow fashion when I wasn't doing it in every category of my life. I began a transition to buying less, using less, and expanding the tenets of my book to areas beyond my craft.

Seasonal Slow Knitting is, in a way, both a deeper and a wider dive into the initial concepts I set forth to be shared and lived. In the pages of this book, I hope that you will discover small ways to change your daily, weekly, monthly, and seasonal knitting practices to make slower crafting a reality for you. I hope that you'll find a single sentence, a tip, or maybe a pattern that resonates and that you can carry with you. And I hope that these words inspire you to continue to make and grow.

about this book

Like *Slow Knitting*, this book is as much about the philosophy behind why we knit, and why we love to create, as it is about following a pattern or working on a project. The book is arranged seasonally, and is designed to guide us through our knitting practice as the weather and world change around us. Whenever you pick up the book and begin reading, I recommend starting with the season that you're in, before reading the whole volume.

Each of the patterns was designed with practicality in mind. I curated a selection of garments, accessories, and home goods that could fill needs and fit seamlessly into any wardrobe and lifestyle. As a result, most patterns are fairly beginner-accessible but should be enjoyable for knitters of any level. I have included notes before each pattern to round out the experience and give helpful advice, so make sure you read them before starting any project.

ABBREVIATIONS

There is a list of abbreviations used for the patterns in the back of this book (see page 187), and a few explanations of techniques mentioned. If you're having trouble with a particular stitch or technique, feel free to look online for related videos or consult other knitting books, or visit my YouTube channel for additional tips and technique guides.

SWATCHING

Swatches are always included in your yardage for the patterns in this book, and you should swatch for pretty much every project in which you care about fit, or where you have the potential to run out of yarn. I typically make swatches measuring about 6 × 6" (15 × 15 cm), without slipping any edges or using any border or flanking stitches. Measure your gauge for garments both unblocked and blocked so that you know how much the fabric grows.

YARN SUBSTITUTIONS & SUGGESTIONS

All the patterns in this book are written for yarns that I find wonderful, and that embody the values I set forth in *Slow Knitting*, but they are far from the only yarns you can use. In each pattern description, I have included other yarns that are equally thoughtful and well suited, and I've tried to offer options that might be more readily available to knitters in countries outside the United States. While shopping for and shipping yarn around the globe is an exciting part of the new normal and has allowed many of us to try new fibers, I've become more aware of how this global marketplace is having an environmental impact. Using yarns made closer to home is a great way to lower your carbon footprint and support local businesses. Feel free to substitute yarns other than the suggestions I've

given—I've also included a description of what makes each yarn ideal or what to look for when swapping one fiber for another.

TIPS & TECHNIQUES

Throughout the book, I share a lot of opinions and suggestions with you about how to do things—or rather, about how I do things. I am no reverse engineer or brilliant mind; I do not claim to have invented or streamlined any process, but have simply found ways that work for me. In sharing my methods for blocking, attaching buttons, or darning, I hope to pass along my way of doing something, such that it might resonate with you.

spring equinox

FRESH AIR

WHILE THE FIRST DAY OF spring is, technically, clearly marked on the calendar, I always feel that the true beginning of spring is the first day warm enough, light enough, and fresh enough to throw open the windows in the house. The sounds of the outdoors are welcome additions to stuffy rooms: Whispery breezes and birds' songs are invigorating and rejuvenating, replacing shadows with sunbeams and coaxing dust bunnies out from their secret warrens.

This breath of fresh air is an exquisite, precious moment. The world casts a rosy glow, aided by cherry blossoms and the appearance of insistent daffodils. There is something so joyful about one of these flowers pushing up in an unexpected place. These tender days make me feel as if a new world, a new year, has truly begun, and I find it odd that the calendar year begins in midwinter (for my hemisphere) or in the center of summer's unforgiving heat (for others). Shouldn't the new year begin at a time when there is so much freshness and transition?

I try to spend as much time as possible out of doors. I have, in recent years, found new delight in working with nature in the form of container gardening. I think it is the concentration and appreciation of materials that have ignited this new interest, and that a settling of my world has allowed me room to focus on tending to growing things. I love selecting little plants to come home and sit beside me in an open window as I write or knit, imagining that they are somehow cheering me on through all efforts as they grow in tandem with my projects.

I have also found that a deep spring cleaning can be extremely rewarding. While I surface-clean all year, spring seems like the right moment to tackle the baseboards, among other things. I find delight in the scents of fresh laundry and a delicate blend of honeysuckle, which replace the heavier scents that fill the closed-up spaces of winter. Similarly, I use this time to clean and prepare my knits for another season. It's time to reward these items for their hard work—an end-of-season sauna for our sweaters, socks, and accessories prepares

them for a cycle of rest before each clean knit is tucked away with care.

The heavy yarns of the past season, plump and comfortable, can be set aside for lighter-spun fibers and a pretty, natural palette. This time of year is my favorite to pull out hand-dyed experiments and dream them into wispy, filigreed confections that call to mind dappled sunshine and delicate new leaves. I am, like my garden, pollinated with new ideas, thoughts, and motivations: an opportunity to refresh and evaluate my practice and projects. Spring is an excellent time to review uncompleted projects languishing in the work-in-progress basket. A good yarn stash rotation also brings new perspective, as does a reorganization of needles and notions, which always seem to find themselves misplaced or entangled after many months. I love discovering a forgotten skein and embracing the excitement of casting on something new, and this feeling is only enhanced by favorite tools placed within easy reach. Embrace this season of beginnings and lean into the idea that it will bring with it a fresh sense of purpose and renewal!

washing your knitwear

WHEN TO WASH

You may be surprised to hear that wool and wool-based projects don't need frequent washing unless they are truly, visibly dirty. Wool is naturally soil-repellent (especially when treated with a lanolized wash); it resists retaining dirt or smells. Your woolen items should be able to be worn many times before needing to be cleaned, especially if you wear them over a lightweight cotton or silk shirt, and not next to your skin. I wash my sweaters fully once a year, and wash socks about once a month, even if I've worn them a few times. Accessories, like shawls, scarves, and cowls, I wash only if they become dirty or soiled with makeup, or begin to take on scents (like perfumes or campfire smells). Mittens, gloves, handwarmers, and hats will depend entirely on their wear—use your judgment, but don't be overzealous! Your handknits will last longer with less stress from washing.

Often, washing large pieces is more effort than I am willing to undertake. If I feel that an item has been exposed to germs (maybe a handknit blanket was used to comfort a sick child), I will steam the garment instead of washing, if it hasn't actually been dirtied. A handheld steamer is a cheap but handy tool, and uses boiling water to generate incredibly hot, sanitizing steam. Hang the item on a clothesline or towel bar, or over the shower bar, and move over it inch by inch with the steamer, held upright, to sanitize the item. You may notice that the piece feels a bit damp afterward, so leave it to dry overnight.

A LAUNDRY LIST

Before you begin, gather some handy items from around the house: a bucket large enough to transport a few of your knits back and forth (especially if you'll be hanging them outside

while they dry, or moving them from one room to another) and a cleansing agent. I have used gentle dish soap from time to time, and I have not had a sock or sweater complain yet.

I love a wool wash with a bit of lanolin, or a nice natural scent like lavender or rosemary, but you can also find many scentless wool washes and soaps, if you have sensitive skin. You'll need somewhere to soak your garments—a deep kitchen sink or clean bathtub is usually my choice—and somewhere to dry things: a clothesline outside or indoors (I have one hanging above my shower stall), a folding clothing rack, or even a nice patio rail, in a pinch. For complex, lacy things that must be shaped, see the section below on "ornate" items and their unique needs (blocking equipment, for instance; see page 117). Additionally, handheld steamers, hangers, and clothespins may be required for some projects.

GENERAL WOOLENS

For socks, sweaters, and accessories that don't require fussy additional attention or special treatment, I take a comprehensive approach, soaking large quantities of woolen items in a single tub or kitchen sink. I'll add about ½ teaspoon (roughly 2.5 ml) of soap per pound (453.5 g), dry, per project (each sock set is typically ¼ pound [113 g]). Fill the basin about halfway with hot water, swishing your hand around in the water to generate some suds and make sure the cleaning agent is well distributed. If you're using a wool wash, you may not have many bubbles—that's okay. Many wool-specific washes are designed to not need rinsing, and that's part of their appeal. After you've drawn the water, dump all your knitted items in together. If any item has a stain that needs some extra attention, apply a bit of soap to a washcloth and dab it on the area, let the soap sit until the water cools, and then run the spot gently under warm water to rinse it out, rubbing it with your fingers but being careful not to scrub (as this might felt woolen yarns).

After everything has soaked for some time and the water has cooled, drain the tub. For projects that you feel need an extra rinse (maybe the water was a bit dirty or dusty, or you feel that the suds from your soap were a bit over-enthusiastic), fill the tub again, this time with lukewarm water, taking care that none of your woolens are underneath the flowing tap. I typically bunch them all up onto the side of the tub, add water until there's enough for a good rinse, and then redistribute the projects throughout. Be careful about moving or agitating especially soft items, as these are likely to felt if given too much vigorous attention.

Once satisfied with the cleanliness of your projects, drain the tub or sink and use your hands to push water out of the pile of woolens until you feel you could carry them somewhere without dripping all over the place. Grab your bucket, pile them in, and take them to the designated drying area.

DRYING SMALL ITEMS

Socks, mittens, hats, cowls, and other smaller knitted items are the easiest to dry. If available, an outdoor clothesline in a shady area is wonderful; if you don't have access to a line, a collapsible clothing rack can be positioned in the best spot on your patio, porch, or balcony. The same collapsible clothing rack is wonderful for indoor use, too, during poor weather. Simply set it up in your bathtub so any drips go down the drain, and turn a fan on if your bathroom has poor ventilation.

DRYING SWEATERS AND LARGER ITEMS

When steaming won't work for them, sweaters, scarves, and shawls that don't need blocking present different drying challenges. I begin prepping them for drying after a bath by pushing out

extra moisture. Roll your piece in an old towel and, using your hands and knees, push more of the water out. The towel protects the knitted item from stretching, while absorbing additional liquid that would take a long time to dry.

Often, heavier pieces are pulled downward by their own weight, creating elongated arms and bodies on sweaters, or long, skinny scarves. To counteract that, a mesh sweater drying frame is handy to have—these are about the size of the top of a washing machine, and can easily be set up at an angle on the back of said machine. They're also handy for use on top of your collapsible drying rack, or can be set up on a table. Just take care to keep them away from cats, who will think you've brought them a handy, wool-lined hammock for afternoon lounging.

If you notice that the position of your piece is stretching it too much in one direction, take the time to reposition it every few hours to keep it from taking on an odd shape during the drying process. A fan, focused on the garment, is almost as effective as a natural, early spring breeze at drying these thicker items quickly.

A NOTE ABOUT SUPERWASH

The appeal of superwash yarns comes from their ability to withstand the abuse of washing machines. These fibers are coated in polymers (plastics) or are chemically treated to remove the scales of the wool, and therefore won't felt. At least in theory—I've seen a few that have felted anyway with rough enough treatment! What's important to note here is that fairly recent research suggests that items that have any synthetic fiber content (like nylon or superwash coating) may be releasing microplastics into our water supply. There is abundant scientific evidence to suggest that washing machines are a major culprit, so if you'd like to wash your superwash items in the washing machine, I recommend hunting down a water-friendly microplastics bag. These bags are made from a new "smart fabric" that traps escaping plastics but allows water to travel freely during the washing process, getting your superwash items clean while keeping them from harming the environment. They come in a size large enough to fit a few cardigans and pairs of socks, and last a very long time, so don't be shy about employing them. (This is a great gift idea for a knitter in your life!)

I would also recommend using these smart bags when washing superwash items by hand, as water that goes down your drain could have plastics in it and get back into our drinking-water source! And while I tend to wash all my handmade pieces by hand, regardless of fiber content, I don't fear throwing superwash items in the dryer for a nice tumble cycle, as that often restores the fiber's shape and structure (the microfiber-trapping bags don't go through the dryer). You can follow these rules for acrylics and acrylic blends, too.

SPECIAL FIBERS

Some fibers are a little more delicate than others and require special treatment and care to look their best! While wool is fairly low-maintenance, alternative animal fibers like alpaca, Angora, cashmere, mohair, and qiviut appreciate some extra attention. Soak these alone in low-suds wool washes, and gently push out remaining water with a towel before laying flat to dry. These fibers don't have the elasticity of wool, so should be laid flat to prevent stretching from which they might not recover. After the item is completely dry, hang it and steam lightly to raise the halo on fibers like Angora, mohair, and Suri.

Judge plant fibers like cotton, bamboo, and hemp based on the finished shape of your garment. (Although it's not a plant fiber, these instructions also apply to silk, and to slinky synthetic fibers). These low-elasticity fibers will be most comfortable drying in their intended final shape. Hang to dry, if you're able to give them adequate support (a hanger, a stretch of clothesline, or a railing are good options). For garments and accessories you would prefer not become elongated, lay flat to dry, or in a zigzag formation across the top of a drying rack. The idea is to take the stress off the fiber, so don't be afraid to reposition if you notice lower areas are retaining moisture while others have dried.

ORNATE, SHAPED PIECES

If you need to wash something that was originally heavily blocked into a shape—items like lace shawls, or anything that required an excessive use of pins on the first go-round—repeat the procedure when drying the freshly washed item. Unfortunately, the yarn won't remember the intricate lace stitches just because it's been in that shape for a year, and you'll need to take the time to remind it with blocking mats and pins.

EMBRACE YOUR EFFORTS

Find small ways to reward yourself throughout the process of washing your knits, and it will never be a chore! Choose wool washes with scents that you find pleasing and soothing. Set aside an afternoon for washing when the weather is nice (for outdoor drying), or choose to immerse your hands and elbows in warm water and woolens on a rainy, gray day. Put on music you enjoy, or get little hands involved, teaching them how to treat handmade things and appreciate the ritual of maintaining an heirloom. Combine your washing efforts with darning and mending, and make a day of it, knocking out a year's worth of tending to your projects in one go while watching a favorite movie. When next you pull out your favorite pair of socks, fresh and ready to be worn, you'll be glad of the time you've put in to keep them going.

blocking accessories

As a new knitter in the early aughts, I wasn't able to simply pop online and ask the internet questions about things I didn't quite understand. When I was starting out, most of my knitting knowledge came from books, many with illustrations or black-and-white instead of color pictures, and none of the books in my library were particularly illuminating about knitting practices in an overarching way. Rather, they were focused on specific project types or techniques, or got into more detail about making an item than they did about finishing it.

As a result, my finishing techniques are all over the place, and I've only recently begun to attempt to firm them up a bit with some better methods and choices. One area in which I found my knowledge to be a bit lacking was the process of blocking accessory pieces of all sizes and shapes. Luckily, I've been able to compile some excellent tips and tricks from other knitters as well as from my own experiences, and I describe them here in hopes that they'll be helpful to knitters of any skill level.

Before we go any further, let me say that for most of my accessory projects I don't believe blocking is an important step, and I think it's okay to skip blocking if your item is one for which it's unlikely to matter if the sizing isn't dead-on. Therefore, my first rule is to block only pieces where fit matters, where the yarn requires it, or where there is lace present. Here are my general rules for blocking different types of items, and some techniques to try should you be inclined. Note that all the blocking I do involves wool and wool blends, and no synthetic materials. Synthetics like acrylic and rayon behave very differently from the fibers I'm familiar with, and you'll need to look elsewhere for instructions for those.

HANDWARMERS, MITTENS, AND GLOVES

These cozy items are likely to block themselves to the perfect fit with just a little wear, and, if overblocked, could very easily stretch out of shape and cease to be useful. I do prefer to knit a swatch before entering into an agreement that any yarn should become a hand item, simply because hands are a lot like feet, and prefer a comfortable, tailored fit over a too-loose one. If you aren't willing to knit a swatch, be ready to wash the first of the pair when it's finished to make sure it doesn't grow massively.

When blocking handwarmers, I often soak for twenty to thirty minutes in warm water, then squeeze out in a hand towel and lay flat or hang over a towel bar to dry. With mittens, you can lay them flat and stuff a bit of plain newsprint into them, to help get a nice round shape without side seams (which look so funny if the mittens are larger, like cartoonish oven mitts). Change the newsprint daily if it takes more than a single day for the mittens to dry, and be careful when using printed paper with light colors, as some inks may transfer to the inside of your mitten if it's light in color.

Mittens that have liners should be dried with the liners unsecured at the peaks of the mittens (the top of your fingers) and pulled out of the mittens (they can remain attached at the cuffs), to increase air flow. If your mitten liner features a yarn with a halo, like alpaca, Angora, or mohair, consider floating an iron on the steam setting above the fabric after everything dries to revive that halo.

If there is lace present in your mitten or handwarmer, it's likely designed to show when your hand naturally stretches the mitten, so there's no major need for blocking. However, if you'd like the lace to show more or you need to

enhance a lace edging, block flat and pin out the edging on a towel or blocking mat.

Gloves, with their individual fingers, do very well using the hang-to-dry method. They can also be steamed, if desired, rather than fully blocked, to retain their shape and settle any weaving-in areas that might be a little lumpy. If you want to do the full block and douse them completely, you can lay them flat to dry and use the mitten newsprint trick.

HATS OF ALL TYPES

I almost never swatch for hats, as it's always been my thought that any hat that doesn't fit me will surely fit someone else, so if it comes out too big or too small, I'll find someone else it belongs to. If you're making a very specific hat for yourself, though, it's always recommended to swatch to make sure that it will fit at the end of the process, especially when yarns that are likely to bloom (like wools and wool blends) are involved.

I avoid blocking hats that fit very close to the head, like beanies, unless they have a stitch pattern designed to open up (like lace, or stranded knitting that needs to even out from tension variations). If you do want to block a beanie hat, be careful not to stretch out the brim when laying it flat to dry, and have a tape measure handy to match the schematic or dimensions provided in the pattern so you don't overstretch and give yourself a larger hat.

For toques, which are designed to have a slightly looser feel, it's possible to pull and stretch the fabric up from the brim and add a little more room, as desired. I typically use a tape measure to pin down my brim to the towel or blocking mat and make sure it isn't stretched before going at the rest of the hat and shaping it with my hands. Often, though, a steam block is all that's needed for a toque, and you can just wear it immediately. Be sure to rotate the hat while blocking to avoid creating fold lines at the sides.

Berets are a funny animal in the hat world, and a lot of fun to block. You'll want to grab a salad plate and a bit of waste yarn to get the best results. First, wet your hat completely and then press out the extra water into the sink and into a towel. After most of the water is out, stretch the hat over the salad plate, with the crown of the beret (the top of the hat) across the bottom of the plate, and the brim in the center on the top of the plate. Take your waste yarn (something not grabby, like a bit of cotton yarn or embroidery floss) and thread it through the brim stitches, then pull them in so that the hat is stretched over the plate, with the brim stitches forming a tight O in the center of the dish. This method opens up lace, shapes stiffer fabrics into that classic shape, and ensures that you'll have a finished hat with a brim that fits.

COWLS

How do you block a circular item that needs to be laid out flat? If your cowl is of the seamed type, you may want to seam it before blocking, to make sure that the seam is less visible, so the rules for blocking cowls are all with a single, circular tube in mind. The exception here is a cowl that has a lace pattern that needs to be blocked flat or pinned out, as it's easier to do this step with a flat piece of fabric.

If your cowl is the small type meant to be worn in a single loop around the neck, and the stitch pattern detail doesn't require precise or heavy blocking (as lace would), you can simply set your iron to the steam setting and get the cowl nice and damp, give it a few pops with your hands to make any uneven tension settle out, and then let it air-dry flat, or over a towel bar. Rotate the piece periodically so that it dries without folds at the sides.

If you've made a single-loop cowl with lace, you can use the towel blocking mat method. First, get as much water out of your cowl as possible, then pull out a fresh hand towel (usually just the right size for those close, single-loop cowls). Begin pinning out the lace pattern against the hand towel, with the hand towel on the inside acting as the blocking mat, and work your way around the circumference of the cowl. Then hang your cowl-with-towel on a peg or bar with the best possible air flow to let it dry completely. Too complex? Use the steaming method and stretch the lace out by hand, pinning only the edges of the cowl and double-layering it on an actual blocking mat—just make sure there's lots of air flow wherever you leave it to dry. As with other circular pieces, rotate it periodically to avoid side folds.

With larger, double-loop cowls, it may be necessary to block lace or fancy stitches flat, as you would a lace wrap or shawl (see below), before seaming. Then you can go back over the seam with an iron on the steam setting or a handheld steamer to help it blend. If your cowl doesn't feature lace, try the steam method first and hang to dry on a hanger or peg, looped as many times as you intend to wear it.

SCARVES AND RECTANGULAR WRAPS

When blocking scarves or rectangular wraps, the amount of precision and work required depends on how large the item is, but also on how important it is for the item to look perfect. If you've got uneven tension issues, or you've done a pattern that would benefit from a good block, go for it, and then hang the piece to dry on a drying rack, or pin it out against your blocking board, interlocking play mats, or a towel. If the piece is too unruly and large to properly pin out but features lace, I recommend skipping the full bath and going straight into blocking using steam. Set your iron to the highest steam setting and fill it up with water, then lay out your piece in sections and let the iron hover above

each section, steaming it and letting it cool completely before pinning out and moving to the next section. It may take you a few days, but this will enable you to give the entire piece a proper block. After you've completed this initial block, you can do a light run over the whole piece with the steam setting so that it looks cohesive.

If you're working with a smaller or less intricate piece of fabric for your scarf or rectangular wrap, feel free to just steam the whole thing hanging and go. In most cases, steaming is enough for a standard scarf or simple wrap.

SHAWLS

Shawls with shapes present new, trickier problems for us as knitters wanting to properly finish our pieces, and require more tools than the average project. Consider investing in blocking wires—thin wires that thread through the borders of your piece and are flexible, to curve and move with elegant shawl shapes. You can anchor these wires to your blocking mats with T-pins, while also saving yourself several hours hunting down every pin you own. For lace shawls, you'll want to wet-block, completely wetting the piece, letting the water cool, then squeezing and pushing the water out so you'll be pinning out the lace damp against your blocking surface. Make sure any unusual shape is completely dry before removing the shawl from your blocking board.

A little blocking can go a long way toward transitioning your knit from having that homemade feel to having a handmade, couture-item feel. Even the simplest fabrics and materials look a little better after being washed. Remember, we handle things a lot while we're making them, and you'd look a bit ragged after twenty to forty hours of handling, too.

Seeds and Stems Cowl

/ About the Yarn /

GARDEN WOOL & DYE CO. LOCAL WOOL: CORMO FINGERING

There's something really special about being able to knit with a yarn whose making you can trace from start to finish. This is the case with Garden Wool & Dye Co.'s Local Wool. While not disclosed on the label, this 100 percent Cormo comes from Dresow Family Farm in Minnesota, which ships the fleeces destined for this yarn to a US mill where they are worked into a delightfully bouncy fingering-weight yarn. The yarn is then sent on to Anastasia Williams, the dyer behind Garden Wool & Dye Co., and natural, botanical color is applied. The yarn I used is dyed with red onion skins to achieve the perfect golden green—one of my favorite colors in any season.

The fabric created by this slightly rustic, 2-ply yarn isn't perfect, but it does have a very nice handspun feel. Each skein I used had slight variations in weight and spin, which is often characteristic of yarns produced by small mills, and this was highlighted by the twisted stitches in the pattern, which already pop out from the fabric. I love the overall effect: Each stem is unique, similar to how each seedling emerging from soil will have its own identity and personality, and this yarn creates a suitably organic backdrop for the lace and cable columns.

SIZES
Single Loop (Double Loop)

FINISHED MEASUREMENTS
25 (50)" [63.5 (127) cm] circumference × 16" (40.6 cm) tall
Note: Measurements are taken unstretched; the fabric is fairly stretchy.

YARN
Garden Wool & Dye Co. Local Wool Cormo Fingering [100% Cormo wool from Dresow Family Farm, Minnesota; 400 yards (366 meters)/4 ounces (100 grams): 1 (2) skein(s) dyed with red onion skins]

ALTERNATIVE YARNS
340 (680) yards [311 (622) meters] in a fingering-weight yarn

If substituting another yarn, look for one that both is lightweight and has good structure. Cormo as a wool fiber has considerable bounce, and good replacements include Targhee, Rambouillet, Merino that has not been superwashed, and other similar wools. Find a woolen-spun yarn with lots of air, if you can, for a truly delicious cowl, or use a worsted-spun yarn for greater stitch definition. The Garden Wool & Dye Co. yarn has a bit of a thick-and-thin quality, which enhances the organic nature of the piece.

(UK) The Little Grey Sheep Hampshire 4-Ply (100% British wool)

(UK) Woolly Mammoth Fibre Co. Natural Sock (50% Bluefaced Leicester wool, 50% Cheviot wool)

(US) Jill Draper Makes Stuff Mohonk Light (100% Cormo wool)

(US) Sincere Sheep Equity Fingering (100% Rambouillet wool)

NEEDLES
One pair straight needles size US 6 (4 mm)

Change needle size if necessary to obtain correct gauge.

NOTIONS

Stitch markers; row counter (optional); blocking pins (optional)

GAUGE

25 sts and 26 rows = 4" (10 cm) in Stems Pattern, blocked, unstretched

PATTERN NOTES

I am not a lace knitter by a long shot, yet I had no trouble getting the rhythm of this allover lace-and-cable pattern after a few repeats. I did use a few little tricks to keep me going, like color-coded stitch markers to help recognize the beginning and end of each stitch pattern, and stitch markers placed between pattern repeats so that I could count how many were complete. The most challenging thing about working the Stems Pattern is that there are so many stitches worked through the back loop. If these give you trouble, look for a needle with a pointy tip, or simply go up in your yarn weight and work one less repeat of the Stems Pattern on each side of the Seed Pods Pattern.

This yarn had minimal bleeding when soaked in warm water with a bit of wool wash, although it was heavy in lanolin and leftover mordant, so I gave it a good swish to try to get some of these oils out. If you find that your skeins are particularly sticky (a common occurrence with naturally dyed yarns), use a gentle, grease-cutting dish soap to cut through some of the oil and release it from the fabric.

SPECIAL ABBREVIATIONS

1/1 LC: Slip 1 stitch to cable needle, hold to front, k1, k1 from cable needle.

1/1 LTC: Slip 1 stitch to cable needle, hold to front, k1-tbl, k1-tbl from cable needle.

1/1 RC: Slip 1 stitch to cable needle, hold to back, k1, k1 from cable needle.

1/1 RTC: Slip 1 stitch to cable needle, hold to back, k1-tbl, k1-tbl from cable needle.

STITCH PATTERNS

Note: You may work the stitch patterns from the written instructions or the charts.

STEMS PATTERN (multiple of 10 sts; 16-row repeat)

Set-Up Row (WS): P1-tbl, k3, p2-tbl, k3, p1-tbl.
Row 1: K1-tbl, p2, 1/1 RTC, 1/1 LTC, p2, k1-tbl.
Row 2: P1-tbl, k2, p4-tbl, k2, p1-tbl.
Row 3: K1-tbl, p1, 1/1 RTC, k2-tbl, 1/1 LTC, p1, k1-tbl.
Row 4: P1-tbl, k1, p1-tbl, p1, p2-tbl, p1, p1-tbl, k1, p1-tbl.
Row 5: K1-tbl, 1/1 RTC, k1, k2-tbl, k1, 1/1 LTC, k1-tbl.
Row 6: P2-tbl, [p2, p2-tbl] twice.
Row 7: 1/1 RTC, k2, k2-tbl, k2, 1/1 LTC.
Row 8: P1-tbl, p3, p2-tbl, p3, p1-tbl.
Row 9: K1-tbl, k2, 1/1 RTC, 1/1 LTC, k2, k1-tbl.
Row 10: P1-tbl, p2, p4-tbl, p2, p1-tbl.
Row 11: K1-tbl, k1, 1/1 RTC, k2-tbl, 1/1 LTC, k1, k1-tbl.
Row 12: P1-tbl, p1, p1-tbl, k1, p2-tbl, k1, p1-tbl, p1, p1-tbl.
Row 13: K1-tbl, 1/1 RTC, p1, k2-tbl, p1, 1/1 LTC, k1-tbl.
Row 14: P2-tbl, [k2, p2-tbl] twice.
Row 15: 1/1 RTC, p2, k2-tbl, p2, 1/1 LTC.
Row 16: P1-tbl, k3, p2-tbl, k3, p1-tbl.
Repeat Rows 1–16 for pattern.

SEED PODS PATTERN (multiple of 10 sts; 16-row repeat)

Set-Up Row (WS): K2, p6, k2.
Row 1: P2, k1, 1/1 LC, 1/1 RC, k1, p2.
Row 2: K2, p6, k2.
Row 3: P2, p6, k2.
Row 4: Repeat Row 2.
Rows 5 and 6: Repeat Rows 1 and 2.
Row 7: P2, k1, yo, ssk, k2tog, yo, k1, p2.
Row 8: K2, p6, k2
Rows 9–16: Repeat Rows 7 and 8.
Repeat Rows 1–16 for pattern.

BEGINNING MEDITATIONS

Work the first row carefully—you're beginning with the wrong side and jumping almost right away into twisted stitches, but the lace in the Seed Pods Pattern doesn't begin until Row 7, so you have a little time to get adjusted before we throw eyelets in there. As stated earlier in the pattern, I used markers of one color to designate the beginning and end of each stitch pattern, and markers of another color between individual repeats of each pattern.

SEED PODS PATTERN

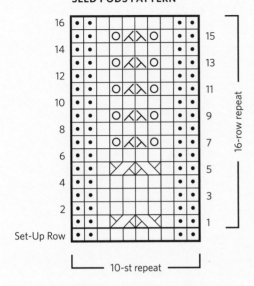

Note: *Chart begins with a WS row.*

STEMS PATTERN

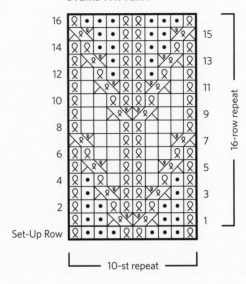

Note: *Chart begins with a WS row.*

☐	Knit on RS, purl on WS.
•	Purl on RS, knit on WS.
ℚ	K1-tbl on RS, p1-tbl on WS.
O	Yo
◿	K2tog
◺	Ssk
⟋	1/1 RC
⟍	1/1 LC
⟋	1/1 RTC
⟍	1/1 LTC

COWL

CO 100 sts.

Set-Up Row (WS): Work Stems Pattern over 40 sts, pm, work Seed Pods Pattern over 20 sts, pm, work Stems Pattern to end.

Work even until piece measures 25 (50)" [63.5 (127) cm] or until you have approximately 4 yds (3.5 m) of yarn left.

BO all sts using the Knitted BO.

FINISHING

Block piece to measurements. Sew CO and BO edges together.

the knitter's dye garden

There aren't many planting guides that are geared toward knitters, and I am far from a plant expert, but I've tried to compile a modest list of plants that have dual purposes. Some satisfy my need for indoor, guilt-free blooms (did you know many of our floral shop purchases come from quite far away?). Others are excellent to have on hand in the kitchen, and almost all of them double as dye plants you can dry, use fresh, or repurpose when wilted. I find that this balance allows for a little plant to go a long way, and I hope you'll give a few of them room to grow.

MARIGOLDS

These sunny, easy-to-grow flowers are cheery and prolific. You can pop the wilted heads off and use them straightaway, or dry them for use later. Get chartreuse on gray or fawn wools, and greenish, golden, or pale yellows on white.

HOLLYHOCKS

These plants are poisonous, so avoid them if you have pets that get too curious (or children, for that matter). Deer and rabbits will generally leave them alone, and the darkest-colored hollyhocks, which are the best for dyeing, are a stunning contrast to yellow dye plants.

AMARANTH

Although the method can be a challenge, amaranth makes beautiful hot pink and even red dyes, and the bold, broom-like flowers are a major pollinator attractant.

HOPI BLACK SUNFLOWERS

This variety of sunflower yields deep blacks and purples, and unused heads can be dried or left for birds in fall and winter. Squirrels will make off with the heads, so you have to monitor them for ripeness!

COSMOS

I love the bright orange variety (because having only yellow flowers doesn't seem like enough fun to me), and the color you get from these delightful blooms is similar in hue.

TANSY

A funny, button-like yellow flower, tansy is used in many herbal remedies to settle stomachs, but should be researched and applied with caution in teas and drinks. As a dye plant, tansy produces a delightfully bright yellow.

ROSEMARY

One of my favorite plants to cook with, rosemary is fragrant and has many uses beyond the kitchen. Combine it in an herbal mix with lavender to tuck into sachets for your yarns and knits in storage, dry it and infuse it into your body products or wool washes, or use it with an iron modifier to get deep silvery tones when natural dyeing.

LAVENDER

Sprigs of lavender make wonderful, lightly scented additions to decor, while dried blooms can be mixed or used alone in sachets. When using lavender for dyeing, expect soft neutrals in the brown and soft pink ranges, despite the purple flowers. You can also infuse body products or wool washes with this beloved scent.

no-grow natural dyes

My entire time spent experimenting with natural dyes has been from an apartment kitchen, with a container-based garden (or no garden at all). I quickly learned that many botanical dye materials don't need to come from the garden. There's a palette of beautiful colors that you can save from the trash can in your kitchen.

Mordanting is the process of bathing your fibers in a metal or another material that will allow them to grab onto color later. You can mordant with store-bought materials like alum (aluminum sulfate), or go a more natural route with rhubarb leaves or (unsweetened, unflavored) soy milk. You can hot-mordant by bringing a bath of the mordant plus dye good (yarn) up to just-below-boiling temperature and simmering for two hours, or you can cold-mordant by immersing your wool with the mordant materials for a week in a bucket or lidded pot. Rhubarb leaves are toxic to plants and people, as are most mordants, so you'll need to have dedicated dye pots, tools, spoons, and measuring cups for this process. Some dye materials, like black tea, won't require any variety of mordant to be picked up by your fabric, making them completely nontoxic and kitchen-safe. You can read more thoroughly about natural dyeing in some of the books I've recommended in the Resources section of this book (see page 190).

BLACK TEA

Summertime in my house means iced tea. While I tend to prefer mine a bit overloaded with sugar, I am getting better, with time, about putting simple syrup in after-brewed tea rather than drinking the four-cups-to-a-gallon sugar-to-tea ratio that I grew up on and love. The added benefit of not brewing with sugar is that it's possible to reuse the tea bags to dye a bit of yarn. Simply soak the tea in hot water for a second "steep" and then allow the yarn to simmer for about an hour or two to affix the color. I've found that four large tea bags (the kind for iced tea) service a single 4-ounce (100-g) skein nicely, and the toasty brown hues are some of my favorites.

COFFEE GROUNDS

The grounds from your French press, percolator, or drip coffee machine don't need to be thrown out immediately! Spread them out on a paper towel or tray to air-dry and save them to make a dye "brew" with later. I got soft taupe tones on a single skein with an alum mordant and a few days' worth of coffee grounds.

TURMERIC

I've experimented with both turmeric root (which looks a bit like yellow ginger root) and turmeric powder, and the powder produces a considerably stronger dye color. A tablespoon (15 ml) dissolved in hot water has the power to dye one or two skeins a bright, sunshine yellow.

AVOCADO PEELS AND PITS

Remove the fruit and wash out your peels and pits, then leave them to dry for a few days in open air, after which you can put them into a container for storage. Save up the pits and peels from six avocados to dye two to three skeins of yarn a range of warm pink, brown, and beige. Increase your quantity for stronger, rosier pinks. While steeping, the water has a slightly evergreen smell, too, which I love.

ONION SKINS

The papery skins of onions—red and yellow—take a long time to save up, but it's well worth the effort when you see the golden yellows, chartreuse greens, and even rich golden browns they can yield. You'll need a weight-for-weight ratio to get enough color (so yes, 4 ounces [100 g] of onion skins equals enough dye for one 4-ounce [100-g] skein).

THE SCENT OF KNITTING

OF ALL OUR SENSES, IT is probably scent that ties us most closely to memories. That has proven true for me, and I still associate certain smells with specific moments in my life. Early on, I found my knitting world absorbed in the smells of lavender oil and dust, of polished wood and long-forgotten bits and bobs of someone else's stash. These scents still carry me back to light-filled rooms with cats in the rafters and the sound of *The Pink Panther* in the background.

Like many crafters who learn to knit at a young age, I put my skills into a period of hibernation while I worked my way through middle and high school, but early in my college years I was in need of something to do with my hands during Iowa's long winters. I found myself at the door of a knitting shop in Des Moines and buying my first skein of hand-dyed yarn, which smelled faintly of vinegar. This rust-colored, chunky wool reintroduced me to knitting and accompanied me as I followed a pattern for the first time, stitch by stitch. Even now, the scent of hand-dyed yarns takes me back to those shelves, the in-wall gas fireplace, and the scent of the shopkeeper's perfume.

When I dove into the yarn industry full-time, I discovered new scents: soft, luxurious wool washes mixed with the scent of damp wool. In my mind, herb sachets and cedar blocks tucked into chests of finished projects mix with the delicate crinkling of tissue paper. As I began to follow my heart and explore slow yarns, I discovered how much I enjoyed the smell of lanolin and hay, the relics left behind in my yarn in the form of vegetable matter. I added patchouli to this repository, from a knitter who makes her own wool washes. And there's the smell of chamomile tea, mixed with spicy wildflower honey, that I drink during my evening knitting time.

Through dyeing, I've discovered even more knitting scents. The smell of boiled plants and flowers is a rich, heady scent, almost like a distillation of time spent walking in the woods or elbows-deep in garden loam. I have embraced the slightly metallic scent of alum-mordanted yarns, the finished, slightly stiffened skeins dried and cured that soon become lofty and soft when rewashed and knit. In the last year, I've traveled more and have cataloged the scents of new places, from the delicate blooms of wild roses pastureside in Montana to the clean, crisp air of a farm in Vermont.

Each of these I hold on to until it grows wispy and thin, only for the associated experience to be revived the next time the scent crosses my path, even thousands of miles away from where I first found it.

Swatch Sachets

I love swatching, but letting go of my knitted swatches seems to be a problem for me. In my studio, it's not uncommon to see little stacks of like-colored swatches piled up on every surface or acting as makeshift coasters for coffee cups. Since I typically buy a single skein of yarn before purchasing enough for a large project, I often have two to three smaller swatches plus a bigger swatch, and after the swatching is done and the project begins, the swatches just become something to store.

While some knitters have been able to solve this problem by sewing swatches into helter-skelter, whimsical blankets, the asymmetry of these projects just doesn't mesh well with my straight-line personality type. And hanging them for decor doesn't really match my style. The truth is, I feel guilty throwing them out! I was never sure of what to do with them—until I started making them into swatch sachets.

The swatch I've used for this tutorial was a large, stranded-knitting swatch, designed to hold up to steeking (cutting), so I was able to cut it up into smaller pieces, around 4" (10 cm) square, to create swatch sachets. However, if you're typically knitting a square or rectangular swatch 5" (12.5 cm) or 6" (15 cm) wide, you can use the swatch as is, with another swatch or a bit of fabric (as shown) for your backing. Fill your sachets with a variety of scents designed to discourage insects and make your knits feel fresher. These also make great additions to any knitted gift, or can stand alone as part of a larger gift basket for loved ones.

MATERIALS

One swatch for the front

One similar-size swatch or cut piece of fabric for the back

Sewing needle, if using a fabric back; tapestry needle, if using two similar-size swatches

Sewing thread, quilting thread, or Pearl cotton, if using a fabric back; weaving yarn, if using two swatches

Scissors

A bit of wool for stuffing

Scented additions: insect-repellent, herbs, and/or essential oils

Begin by prepping your swatch and the backing material to match in size. Swatches with a tight fabric work better than swatches with a loose gauge, and openwork swatches (featuring lace) are a no-go for this project.

Holding both pieces with right sides together, whipstitch around the outer edge of the entire square, leaving a 1" (2.5 cm) gap between your beginning and ending points. Leaving

your yarn or thread attached and the needle threaded, turn the sachet right side out so that the seams are on the inside.

Prepare the filling (I used a bit of wool left over from a spinning project as batting) by adding a few drops of essential oil to the wool to create a heavily scented sachet, or pull the wool apart and add some herbs between the bits. Stuff the sachet to the desired fullness.

After filling, use your fingers to gingerly turn in the edges at the gap and stitch it closed, keeping the seam to the inside. Secure your stitching with a knot and pull it through the fabric, into the pillow. When you push your needle back out, pull it tight and clip the tail close to the fabric. When you release it and fluff the pillow, it should pull the end into the sachet, leaving you with clean edges and no ends.

Toss your sachet into a drawer or wool-storage bin to help deter insects, or add a sachet to your lingerie drawer and spray it with your favorite perfume. You can revive your sachets each season with a few drops of essential oils placed directly on the fabric.

WOOL-SAVING SCENTS

We've all heard the horror stories of knitters who uncovered a bit of stash or a beloved project only to discover that something pesky and horrible had eaten away at it. There are many pests that enjoy a bit of wool, especially if unwashed and well-worn, for a midafternoon snack or nesting material, so it's important to store our woolens clean and safely away from tiny creatures that might plot their demise.

CEDAR

Now a highly coveted item, cedar chests were for hundreds of years a must-have for textile storage, thanks to their insect- and vermin-repellent properties. This heavily scented wood can be a bit strong for those who are sensitive to smells, and for those of us who can't find the space or budget for a cedar chest, cedar blocks and planks are easy to come by and serve just as well when added to a plastic tub or dresser drawer.

LAVENDER

Lavender is known to repel moths, as well as or better than mothballs, with a lighter scent that doesn't call to mind your great aunt's closet. This floral is readily available in dried form, already removed from the stalk, so it's easy to stuff into fabric sachets that freshen up drawers. I also love both the aesthetic and the scent of lavender and herbs gathered into bouquets, dried hanging upside down, and then added to the back of a closet for extra repellent properties.

ROSEMARY

Rosemary is a strongly scented herb that is useful outside the kitchen and also does duty as a dye plant (see page 27)! I love it for sachets because the scent is earthy and fresh, and blends well with lavender. The woody stalks of rosemary hold up nicely during drying and don't shed the way bundles of lavender do. You can also strip the herb from the stem and mix it into a sachet.

CATCH AND RELEASE

FINISHING IS A BIG PART of knitting. Regardless of your stance as a process or a project knitter, when we begin a new project, from the first moment we cast on, there is some idea in our minds that we will finish, that a final stitch will be bound off, and our knitting will *become something*. Having made things many times over, we carry this knowledge of the eventual finishing into our buying process: We know that we are capable of turning a raw material into something beautiful, so we assume we'll do so with each and every skein we buy.

In reality, many of us are drowning in stash. We hide yarn away in closets, in boxes, or under the bed. We recycle endless empty jokes online about sock stash not counting toward our total and about SABLE: stash acquisition beyond life expectancy. We pull the trigger on purchase after purchase while ignoring the looming problem that surrounds us. It's possible, as a maker, to write off materials without acknowledging that they can easily become a placating shopping addiction of their own. There is something comforting and wonderful about buying yarn and wool. It makes us happy—until it doesn't.

Sometimes, yarn comes into our lives without the intention of ever *becoming* anything. What it is to us isn't yarn at all, in the sense that to be knit or crocheted is not its purpose. It has become hope in a moment of despair, a spark of joy at a time that we needed it most. Maybe the softness of a single Merino skein is a comfort after the loss of a family member, friend, or beloved pet. A vibrant skein reminds us of color in a world that has felt gray day after day. It is celebrated in that moment, a welcome relief from a mundane day, and then moves into storage.

If you find that you have been following unhealthy patterns in buying yarn, spring is the perfect time to reevaluate and tackle the issue. The freshness of the world in this season, an increase in daylight and pretty days, gives us the opportunity to air out our rooms and our thoughts, and start fresh. The ability to take a break, go for a walk, and rejuvenate ourselves in the sunshine is key to success when sorting through the emotions we've

invested in, and the relationships we've built with, yarns in our stashes.

It is our job, as if these yarns are individual sheep we have collected, to take stock and determine which yarns are ready to be shepherded into new lives, new homes, and new hands. Maybe we are ushering them into the unknown, through donation or sale, but we can also shuffle them into the hands of a friend, an eager young knitter, or someone on a budget tighter than our own who will turn them into stitches and projects sooner than we can. Whether you are letting go because a phase in your own knitting cycle has ended (goodbye, hot-pink speckle skein), or because your crafting goals have transitioned to projects for which the yarn is not suited, do not feel guilty.

It does not dishonor the yarn, or the money that was spent on it, to transition it into a new life. Don't require that you recoup funds for every purchase you've made. Although you're welcome to attempt to sell stash, realistically you know that a dollar-for-dollar return is unlikely, especially if the yarn in question has gone out of vogue. Trends fade. We should feel no more guilty moving on from a skein of ruffle yarn than we do from a pair of pastel, pleather pants—and we shouldn't expect other knitters or crocheters to be eagerly embracing trends that are over and done with, either.

Keep only what gives you hope, inspiration, and excitement. Think of your stash as the most magical of yarn shops: perfectly curated by you, in tune with your tastes, and ready to cast on at a moment's notice. This ensures that, in the projects you make, you're more likely to use the stash you have, instead of acquiring more.

rotating your stash

Some of us define stashing as collecting yarns in advance of being able to use them. Like having a pantry stocked with dry staples and spices, having a stash full of yarns that you love that are ready to go for a project at a moment's notice allows you to skip a trip to the yarn shop or avoid waiting for new yarn to arrive in the mail. For many of us, however, our stash can become a sumptuous feast for pests. Did you know that there are pesky little critters in this world who exist solely to damage our beautiful, curated yarn collections? Avoiding moths, carpet beetles, and mice, along with dust mites and sun exposure, is the best reason to rotate your stash regularly.

There are other reasons for (and benefits of) frequent stash rotation. One of these is to cull and curate what we have for future use. Cycling through and organizing our stashes, and refreshing our memories about what lives within our yarn collections, can be the best way to rejuvenate ideas and excitement about yarn we already have on hand, in turn helping us resist the urge to keep buying and filling up our spaces. I am a firm believer in the "love the one you're with" approach to yarn shopping, and even when my tastes change I attempt to compensate by assigning stash yarns to new projects that suit my present state.

Of course, beginning is often the hardest part: Who among us has not thrown open a closet or cupboard, or peeked under the bed, and felt hopelessly overwhelmed by the amount of yarn in residence? Upon closer inspection, it is almost never organized into neat piles according to weight. The practice of organizing and rotating one's stash is often an exhausting, messy, and time-consuming affair, but when accomplished is one of the most rewarding processes we can pursue.

There are many groups online devoted to "cold sheeping" it—going cold turkey on buying, and knitting only from stash. I think that while this is a great idea in theory, digging around in a stash that overwhelms you, or trying to figure out a project to use yarn you feel lackluster about, isn't going to help you move forward with this goal. Before cutting yourself off from buying new yarn, it's a good idea to take inventory. To begin, you'll want to pull everything you have out into view so that it can be evaluated for viability, damage, and your needs. Yes, I mean the skeins in the garage, in the attic, and under the bed. I want you to bring them all into a single, clean room and go through them box by box, tub by tub, yarn store bag by yarn store bag. If you are concerned about possible mouse or insect damage in any part of your stash, don't mingle your skeins; work only with yarns that have been stored together, one group at a time.

Now that you know what you have (and how you feel about it), it's time to make judgments on that yarn. Divide the yarns into piles or bins based on how they make you feel. Skeins in wonderful condition with tags that can be resold, singles that are destined to become hats, or even donations—move them to an appropriately labeled box, tub, or basket. Group skeins destined for large projects together so they can be located when the time comes (I store my sweater quantities on shelves so that I can see what my future wardrobe will look like!). Take a businesslike approach: If the yarn is more than a year old, it can be written off as a loss, and you've already paid the emotional and mental "taxes" on it. If you have a lot of "donation"-designated yarns that you feel other knitters would love, have a stash swap with friends—but don't feel like you have to take anything home. Bring the yarn in with the idea that if you can't find something that you love to swap for, you'll give your yarn away. If it goes unnoticed by your knitting friends, *then* donate it to a nursing home, charity shop, or local craft center.

Partial balls are the bane of my existence (and possibly yours, too?). I try to store partials of similar weights together, and keep only partials that are above a certain weight, unless they are colorwork-worthy partials that could be used together in a project.

A digital, visual inventory system like Ravelry's stash feature is a wonderful tool you can employ throughout this organization process. It allows you to note, and search, things like where you've stored the yarn (tub, garage, attic, spare closet, etc.) and how much yardage you have.

Recording your stash on Ravelry is handy when looking for patterns that match your yarn, too. Store the actual yarns in a way that makes sense for your location, weather, and needs. Remember that yarn is often made from natural fibers that won't do well if locked in a plastic bin or bag in a hot attic or garage (think of what happens to your own hair when it's overheated). If you intend to store your yarns in an open cube wall or shelving so you can view them, be sure that you turn the skeins frequently to prevent strong sunshine from fading the outward-facing bits.

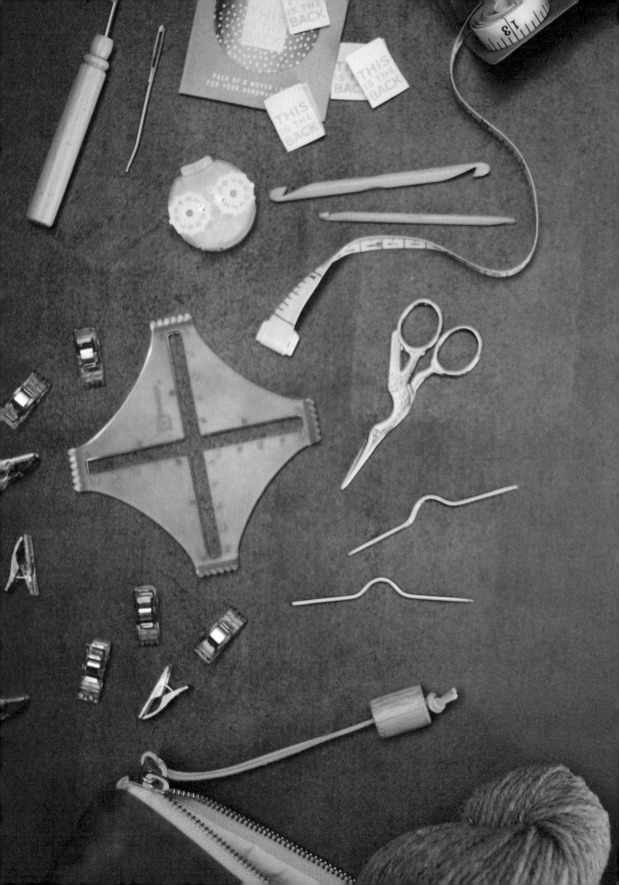

notions organization

Whether intended to be functional, useful, or simply delightful, the large variety of tools available to us is one of the joys of being a knitter. With each year, new and innovative solutions to long-term problems, or updates to must-have tools, find their way onto the market and into our notions stashes, to be tested, measured against their predecessors, and carried along with projects. Notions do present a variety of storage challenges, given the width and breadth of the category.

For high-use items like scissors, I tend to prefer open, easily accessible storage options. In my studio, I have a shelving unit with hooks on the bottom wonderfully suited to scissors, and I store by size so that I can easily grab a pair to use immediately or toss into a project bag, and return without fuss. Other items I might store in the open include tape measures (wind one in a figure-eight shape around your fingers and you can also hang it from a hook), darning eggs and mushrooms, and decorative yarn bowls.

Most notions, however, are small. Stitch markers, the tiniest of all knitting notions, can be a challenge to store (and to keep away from the mouths of pets and children). I have found that pill boxes are an excellent solution for decorative, larger stitch markers, and I store tiny, ring-style markers in a sliding-lid metal or wooden box. My father has a liking for wooden boxes designed to hold guitar picks, and they're just the right size for ten to twelve of the small, ring-style markers you might want to take along for a sweater project. Small notions that get less use (like buttons) are perfectly homed in small glassine bags. These paper bags are translucent, and it's easy to find what you're searching for without excessive digging. Line them up in an old recipe box.

Bent-tip tapestry needles are must-haves for me, and I never seem to have enough of them on hand. Some brands ship them ready for storage in capsule-like containers, but you can purchase wooden needle cases with plugs that are a bit prettier from embroidery and sewing sources. The brand Cocoknits, founded by knitting designer Julie Weisenberger, has several solutions for tapestry needle and small object storage, from a metal slap bracelet that keeps your needles and pins handy while you're blocking or seaming to an accessory roll (which I could certainly no longer function without).

I recommend keeping blocking-related items together—a long tube is wonderful storage for blocking wires and a yardstick, and can stack nicely in the back of a closet or be positioned upright in an umbrella stand by your studio door (an excellent excuse to look for pretty umbrella stands in vintage shops!). Umbrella swifts also store well this way, if you aren't able to install them permanently on a table.

Project bags, which I love and of which I seem to have an endless supply, I store in a sturdy, drawer-like box, but a milk crate or vintage wooden crate would also serve well. The stiffer bags I stand up, with smaller, muslin-style drawstring ones folded and tucked inside. What might look like four in-use project bags is actually closer to fifteen, thanks to this space-saving system. (A series of hooks in the back of a closet or on the wall is perfect for storing projects in progress, too.)

For unwieldy or oddly shaped notions, I adore the clean look of fabric-covered photo boxes. Many of these boxes come with slide-in, write-on labels that are useful for cataloging their contents. My photo boxes store needle gauges, row counters, the pill boxes I use for my stitch markers, pom-pom makers, and similar items.

needle storage

I have an abundance of interchangeable sets, an inheritance of straight needles, and a wealth of double points that have been gifted and purchased for various projects, and so needle organization has become both a vital need and a daunting task. Despite my best efforts, knitting needles transform from sets of five to sets of four, turn up in my hair and handbags and under beds, and never seem to be in the right place when I go looking for them. Needle (and hook) storage is a must for any crafter, and if you start concerning yourself with it early, you'll spend less time hunting and more time making.

INTERCHANGEABLES

Most interchangeable sets now seem to come with their own container systems, whether a plastic pouch with a slide-in spot for each needle tip and a zippered case for the cords and accoutrements, or a fancy, sewn leather pouch. Although I think these are lovely in theory, I've found that my interchangeables naturally migrate from one case to another, being friendly as they are, so I store them all together in a single pouch designed for interchangeable sets. Mine comes from Chic-a, a company in Mexico dedicated to making knitters' storage tools. It

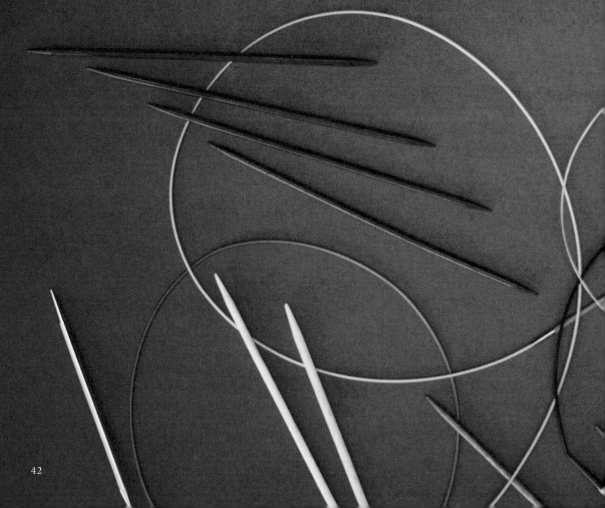

has short sleeves for the various tip sizes and a single, central zippered pouch where I store the cords and connectors.

CIRCULAR NEEDLES

The smartest way to store circular needles is the way yarn stores do: either on pegboard or in drawers, each needle in the individual envelope it came in. Circular needle manufacturers have already done the work for us by creating durable packaging materials that have all the information clearly printed on them, and you can keep the envelopes filed in a drawer in the same fashion you'd store greeting or index cards.

It would be nice if I was clever enough to implement this system in reality, but unfortunately most of my needles no longer have their original packaging. Here, a hanging needle holder with individual, horizontal sleeves for longer cords, and pockets for shorter cords, can serve as a beautiful and functional addition to your craft space. I've also seen photos in which a series of hooks on the wall serves as needle storage, if you have the wall space.

DOUBLE-POINTED NEEDLES

There are abundant needle storage options available for those who use double-pointed needles! From slide-in cases to shoe boxes to photo storage boxes, it's easy to find horizontal storage for your double-point sets. Band them together using small hair elastics, or bring them into open storage: Collect Mason jars or pretty vintage vessels to display them on a shelf. Label your jars with tags or adhesive labels to make the needles you need easier to find in a flash. Some of the newer needle brands are even color-coding their sizes now, making it simple to identify same-size needles when you don't have a needle gauge handy.

STRAIGHT NEEDLES

I am not a knitter who actively works on straight needles anymore (I prefer circular needles for their ability to be folded into project bags), but I do have a beautiful collection of them from my grandmother, who had a brief foray into knitting Aran sweaters. I have always felt that straight needles look exceptionally lovely in handmade pottery, and if you're not a flower person, this is an opportunity to put a vintage vase to good use. As for me, I have a slab-formed, vertical clay "box" with a lid that I find pleasantly hides the needles and protects them.

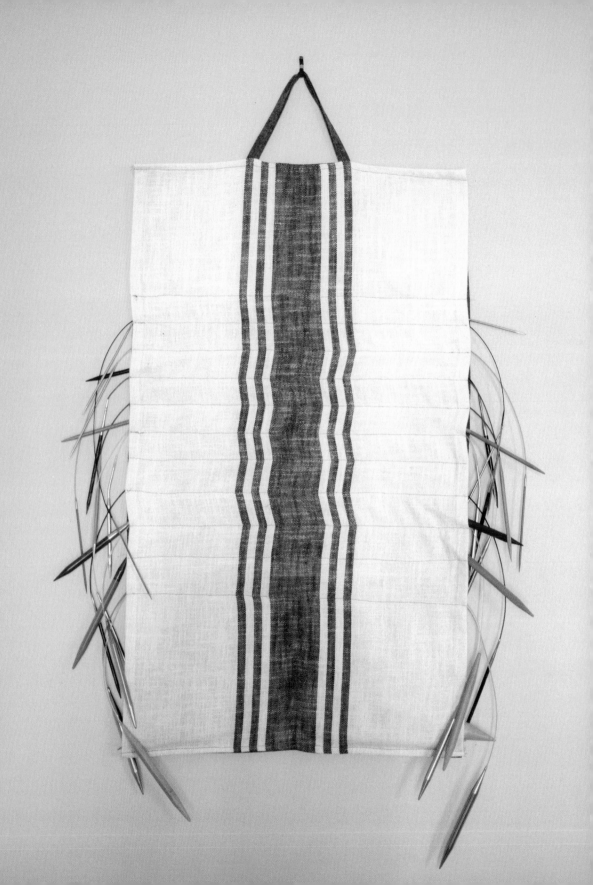

Hanging Circular Needle Storage

Some time ago, I visited a knitting friend who had made herself a hanging, pocketed storage solution for her circular needles. While it was hardly a new idea, the holder was clever and easily hidden on the back of a studio door, and I thought I could sew one up later for my own use. I've finally devised a way to create one of these, and was pleased to discover that the project takes about an afternoon. You need a sewing machine and a bit of sewing experience.

MATERIALS

One piece of medium-weight cotton or linen fabric for the front, 17 × 30" (43 × 76 cm). For simplicity, I used prepared tea towel fabric that already has the side seams finished, making it 16" (40.5 cm) wide preseamed.

One piece of similar fabric for the back, 17 × 30" (43 × 76 cm). I used a cotton-linen blend.

One piece of home-decor-weight interfacing, nonfusible, 16½ × 30" (42 × 76 cm)

One piece of fabric for the loop, 2 × 10" (5 × 25.5 cm). This piece can be made from the same fabric as either the back or the front; it is the hanging loop for your needle holder, so choose a fabric with some sturdiness.

Scissors or a rotary cutter for trimming your fabric

Transparent quilting ruler or yardstick

Cutting mat or smooth cutting surface. (A cutting mat is a must if using a rotary cutter.)

Fabric marking pen or quilter's chalk

Straight pins or quilting clips

Cotton thread in a color to match your fabric

An iron and ironing board, set up and ready to use on a setting appropriate to your fabric choices

If you are using a toweling fabric, your side seams have already been prepared for you. If you are using standard fabric without pre-seamed edges, turn a ¼" (6 mm) edge over on both long sides of the fabric, pin the edge with straight pins or clip it with quilting clips, as shown, sew in place and iron it flat.

For the front piece (if not using preseamed toweling fabric), fold the first seam over once more for another ¼" (6 mm) edge, to completely seal in the raw edge of the fabric, and sew in place. For the back piece, lay the interfacing against the back fabric, matching edge to edge, then flip ¼" (6 mm) over and sew the interfacing to the back piece. Both pieces should now be of equal size—16½ × 30" (42 × 76 cm).

Take your 2 × 10" (5 × 25.5 cm) fabric and fold each long side into the center, as if making bias tape. Press, then fold again to enclose the raw edges. Sew a seam along the long, open side of the tube to seal it up.

Line up the top and bottom fabrics with the right sides together, taking time to make sure that the lengths are equal, and cleaning up any uneven edges at the top or bottom with your scissors. It's okay if you need to lose a little length here, as it will not drastically affect your finished project; just make sure the edges are straight.

Sandwich your hanging loop strip in between the layers of fabric, lining it up with the center of the fabric, with a space of about 4" (10 cm) between the ends of the loop where they meet the raw edge of the front piece.

Lay the back piece down again to form the top of the sandwich, then carefully move the pins so they are holding both layers of fabric and the hanging loop fabric in place for sewing.

Add pins as desired along the top (wide) side of the fabric to secure it while sewing the top edge.

Sew ½" (1.3 cm) in from the top edge to secure the seam.

Turn the top seam inside out and press to make the edge nice and flat.

Turn it right side out again. Sew the bottom edges together in the same way, omitting the sandwich and loop instructions, then turn the piece right side out so that the seams and interfacing are inside the piece.

Using your quilting ruler or yardstick and the fabric marker or quilter's chalk, mark off where you want the lines for the various pockets to go. For a horizontal needle pocket, you'll want between 1¼" (3 cm) and 1½" (4 cm) of space between the lines. To make a vertical division in a pocket (perfect for storing short-corded circular needles), mark a center line down the back of the needle holder, then a horizontal line. Sew each line carefully, alternating which edge of the fabric (left or right) you begin on to avoid shifting.

Your needle holder is finished! Use an iron to press any seams flat, then begin adding the needles to their new home.

You can hang your needle holder from a hook on the back of a door or a nail on the wall, or on the inside of a cabinet.

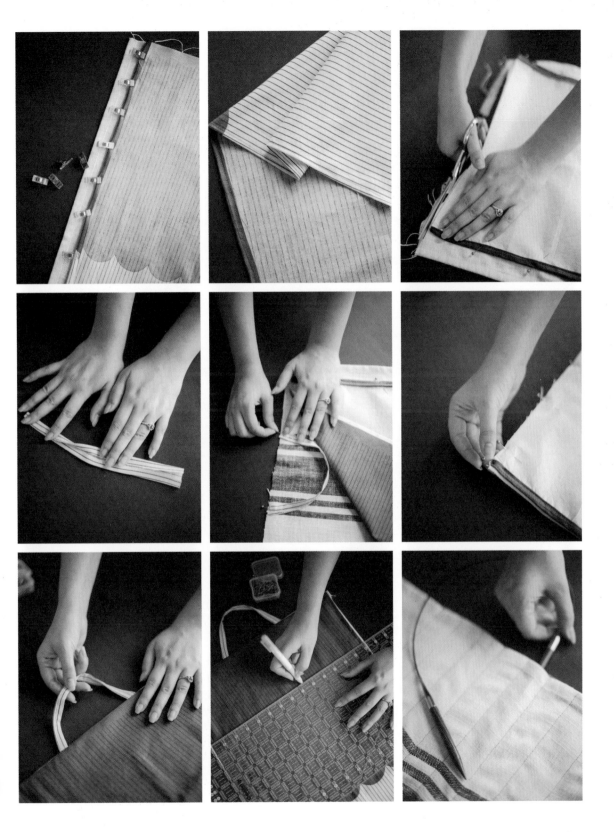

Heirloom Chevron Baby Blanket

/ About the Yarn /

FANCY TIGER CRAFTS: HEIRLOOM ROMNEY

I always challenge knitters who are helping to welcome a new baby to stretch their notion of what makes a good baby yarn. In fact, babies and young children have yet to develop preferences in regard to texture, and the world is their oyster. All too often we pamper babies with the softest materials we can find, which actually works against a lifelong love of wool. Being exposed to a variety of textures helps us become more readily accepting of different materials we might encounter as adults. With this baby blanket pattern, I want to urge you to consider all the benefits of a slightly rough wool.

Jeane deCoster, a true champion of US-produced wool and the owner-operator of Elemental Affects, worked with Fancy Tiger Crafts and a Romney wool ranch in California to develop the Heirloom Romney yarn used for this pattern. Heirloom Romney certainly lives up to its name: Romney is a durable longwool that has a beautiful luster and halo. This yarn is produced—from sheep to skein—entirely in the United States and comes in a fabulous variety of colors that suit any modern nursery, with plenty of selling points to help you convince questioning parents.

Since Romney is a longwool, it doesn't felt easily and can withstand chewing, drooling, and epic amounts of handling. Even better, it will look good through all of it, developing a slightly loftier halo and a softer hand over time. For parents concerned about washing, this Romney can withstand a delicate cycle and even a low-heat tumble dry without major shrinkage, and it can even tolerate a little scrubbing of isolated stains.

SIZES
Crib (Throw)

FINISHED MEASUREMENTS
31¾ (49¾)" [80.5 (126.5) cm] wide × 40 (70)" [101.5 (178) cm] long, after blocking, unstretched

YARN
Fancy Tiger Crafts Heirloom Romney [100% US Romney wool; 200 yards (183 meters)/

4 ounces (112 grams)]: 4 (12) skeins Natural

ALTERNATIVE YARNS
890 (2,435) yards [690 (2,235) meters] in a heavy worsted-weight yarn

If substituting another yarn, look for something that has good drape, as particularly round yarns will make for a dense blanket. If you want to use something with more bounce, you may want to try getting gauge on a DK weight.

(Canada) Julie Asselin Nurtured (100% wool [Rambouillet, Targhee, and Merino])

(France) De Rerum Natura Gilliatt (100% Merino wool)

(US) Jill Draper Makes Stuff Rockwell (100% Cormo Merino crossbred wool)

(US) Stone Wool American Cormo (100% Cormo wool)

NEEDLES

Size US 9 (5.5 mm) circular needle, 40 (60)" [100 (150) cm] long

Change needle size if necessary to obtain correct gauge.

NOTIONS

Removable stitch marker; row counter (optional); yarn for lifelines (optional); blocking pins (optional)

GAUGE

16 sts and 20 rows = 4" (10 cm) in St st, wet-blocked

PATTERN NOTES

A circular needle is used to accommodate the large number of stitches.

This blanket uses some pretty basic techniques and is suitable for a beginning knitter, but you'll need to pay attention, as the Elongated Chevron pattern takes a few rows to develop and isn't always intuitive. I found that it wasn't much use placing stitch markers between repeats, as the pattern shifts every few rows and throws the markers off, requiring you to move them.

A row counter might be handy. Some lifeline yarns could also help if you have trouble counting rows (insert after each full repeat of the pattern over 16 rows.)

Stitch hint: The easiest way to understand this stitch pattern is to read your stitches. The even rows are lined up the same as the wrong side rows, but they are knits instead of purls. The pattern

repeats for 4 rows, then switches. Pay the most attention on Rows 1, 5, 9, and 13, where the pattern switches. In the rest of the rows, just knit the knits and purl the purls.

A note on joining new skeins: This yarn doesn't felt easily, and so it isn't a good candidate for the Felted Join. It does, however, work beautifully with a Russian Join (see Special Techniques, page 188). I recommend using a join instead of simply weaving in your ends since children seem to have a tendency to find loose strings and pull on them.

STITCH PATTERN
ELONGATED CHEVRON
(multiple of 18 sts + 1; 16-row repeat)

Row 1 (RS): P1, *[k2, p2] twice, k1, [p2, k2] twice, p1; repeat from * to end.

Rows 2–4: Knit the knit sts and purl the purl sts as they face you.

Row 5: *[P2, k2] twice, p3, k2, p2, k2, p1; repeat from * to last st, p1.

Rows 6–8: Repeat Row 2.

Row 9: K1, *[p2, k2] twice, p1, [k2, p2] twice, k1; repeat from * to end.

Rows 10–12: Repeat Row 2.

Row 13: *[K2, p2] twice, k3, p2, k2, p2, k1; repeat from * to last st, k1.

Rows 14–16: Repeat Row 2.

Repeat Rows 1–16 for pattern.

BEGINNING MEDITATIONS

While casting on for the blanket, try to keep your hands relaxed so that each stitch is fairly evenly

pulled, but don't pull too tight. You want an edge that can flow and stretch, not an edge that pulls the pattern inward. Given the number of stitches, I recommend casting on in a quiet place. You'll have plenty of time to watch your favorite shows while knitting on this blanket once the stitch pattern becomes familiar to you.

For now, concentrate on the sheer wooliness of this beautiful yarn: the feel of it in your hands, the simultaneous roughness and softness, the slightly heathery texture of all the natural Romney fibers blended together. Think about the sheep in California on the Tawanda Farms who were originally bred just for this yarn. If you're working with a dyed colorway, think about the beautiful color that you've selected, and notice the nuances in every stitch you cast on. Count the cast-on number and count it again, then turn your work and begin.

Once you have begun working the stitch pattern, if you must stop mid-row, try to stop at the end of one repeat and before the start of another. If you can get into that habit, the blanket will be easier to pick up later.

When binding off stitches, take your time and rest the bulk of your (now heavy) project on your lap or a table so that it isn't pulling on you while you're performing your bind-off. Don't pull the stitches too tight or they will tug the blanket inward at the top.

ELONGATED CHEVRON

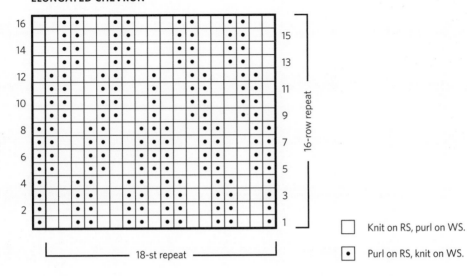

Knit on RS, purl on WS.

• Purl on RS, knit on WS.

18-st repeat

16-row repeat

BLANKET

Using the Knitted CO, CO 127 (199) sts, making sure CO is worked with a relaxed hand and isn't tight.

Begin Elongated Chevron, placing a marker near the beginning of the first RS row to mark the RS of the piece; work even until piece measures 40 (70)" [101.5 (178) cm] from the beginning, or to desired length, leaving approximately 3 (6) yards [2.7 (5.5) meters] for the BO row.

BO all sts using the Knitted BO.

FINISHING

Block piece to measurements.

I have tested this yarn in the washing machine on the cool-water, delicate cycle, and found that it had no problem at all enduring a trip through the machine, and then tumbling dry on low until it was fluffy and light. Make sure you don't use any kind of bleach, and certainly not Woolite (which, despite the name, isn't meant for woolens). If you want the blanket to look pristine and your stitches crisp, I recommend laying flat to dry instead of tumbling, so that you can pin out the edges and make the corners sharp. The washing machine's spin cycle will have done most of the work of getting the water out for you. If the blanket gets badly stained, it's possible to spot-treat this durable wool by rinsing and gently scrubbing the stain with a bit of dish soap or wool wash.

High Relief Baby Blanket

/ About the Yarn /

KELBOURNE WOOLENS: GERMANTOWN

Having lost both of my grandmothers at a young age, as a child I would often daydream about what it would be like to have a grandmother with a button, yarn, or fabric stash. I thought of being able to turn to an older knitter for advice or opinions on material, technique, or construction. As I grew older, I discovered that these women, although not related to me by blood, were all around me, in the quilters, sewists, knitters, and crocheters I met through craft fairs and community groups, the library, and parents' friends.

Better than simply having a friend with the benefit of years of expertise is having a friend who also has a meticulously maintained stash that she allows you to explore—and occasionally shop for your next project! One of my favorite things to discover in a stash is yarn that has been passed down and continues from hand to hand with the hope that it will someday be used: sensible center-pull logs, adorned with faded labels that proclaim "100% virgin wool"— the kind you can imagine buying and bringing home for your first knit.

Kelbourne Woolens has magically captured the aesthetic of knitting in the 1940s to 1970s, translated in a way that a knitter of any age can appreciate. This spongy, delightful wool comes in a range of colors from mustard to brilliant turquoise, and each color is fleece-dyed for evenness, making this an excellent choice for larger projects that may go beyond a single dye lot. This yarn is also excellent for knitters of any skill level, as it has surprising elasticity.

SIZES
Crib (Throw)

FINISHED MEASUREMENTS
26¾ (51¾)" [68 (131.5) cm] wide by 39½ (79½)" [100.5 (202) cm] long, unstretched, after blocking, not including fringe

YARN
Kelbourne Woolens Germantown [100% US wool; 220 yards (201 meters)/3.5 ounces (100 grams)]: 4 (14) skeins Natural, with and without fringe

ALTERNATIVE YARNS
If replacing with another yarn, look for something that has a round and plump strand; the loose gauge of this blanket keeps it soft and cuddly, but with a less structured yarn the texture will be lost. A multi-plied yarn also ensures less unraveling for your fringe and a piece that will hold up as a hand-me-down. I would consider the Germantown to be a lighter worsted weight, so it may be easily replaced here with a thicker DK-weight yarn.

790 (3,040) yards [722 (2,780) meters] in worsted-weight yarn, including fringe; 775 (3,010) yards [709 (2,752) meters] without fringe

(UK) Blacker Yarns Blacker Swan Falklands Merino Blend DK (100% Falkland Island Merino and Shetland wool)

(US) Barrett Wool Co. Home (100% American wool)

(US) Quince & Co. Lark (100% American wool)

NEEDLES

Size US 11 (8 mm) circular needle, 32" (80 cm) long or longer

Change needle size if necessary to obtain correct gauge.

GAUGE

14 sts and 20 rows = 4" (10 cm) in Diamonds, wet blocked

PATTERN NOTES

A circular needle is used to accommodate the large number of stitches.

Before working the edging, the side edges may look a bit wonky due to the changes in stitch texture and pattern. This is okay—the garter stitch edge will even that out. Resist the urge to slip the first stitch of any row, as this makes it harder to pick up stitches accurately from the edge.

STITCH PATTERNS

Note: You may work the following patterns from the written text or the charts.

TRIANGLES A

(multiple of 12 sts + 1; 11-row pattern)

Set-Up Row (WS): P6, *k1, p11; repeat from * to last 7 sts, k1, p6.

Row 1: K6, *p1, k11; repeat from * to last 7 sts, p1, k6.

Row 2: P5, *k3, p9; repeat from * to last 8 sts, k3, p5.

Row 3: K5, *p3, k9; repeat from * to last 8 sts, p3, k5.

Row 4: P4, *k5, p7; repeat from * to last 9 sts, k5, p4.

Row 5: K4, *p5, k7; repeat from * to last 9 sts, p5, k4.

Row 6: P3, *k7, p5; repeat from * to last 10 sts, k7, p3.

Row 7: K3, *p7, k5; repeat from * to last 10 sts, p7, k3.

Row 8: P2, *k9, p3; repeat from * to last 11 sts, k9, p2.

Row 9: K2, *p9, k3; repeat from * to last 11 sts, p9, k2.

Row 10: P1, *k11, p1; repeat from * to end.

LEFT-SLANTING RIB

(multiple of 4 sts; 4-row repeat)

Row 1 (RS): *K2, p2; repeat from * to end.

Row 2: K1, *p2, k2; repeat from * to last 3 sts, p2, k1.

Row 3: *P2, k2; repeat from * to end.

Row 4: P1, *k2, p2; repeat from * to last st, p1.

Repeat Rows 1–4 for pattern.

DIAMONDS

(multiple of 8 sts + 1; 8-row repeat)

Row 1 (RS): K5, *p1, k7; repeat from * to last 6 sts, p1, k5.

Row 2: K1, p3, *k1, p1, k1, p5; repeat from * to last 7 sts, k1, p1, k1, p3, k1.

Row 3: K3, *p1, k3; repeat from * to last 4 sts, p1, k3.

Row 4: K1, p1, *k1, p5, k1, p1; repeat from * to last st, k1.

Row 5: K1, *p1, k7; repeat from * to last 2 sts, p1, k1.

Row 6: K1, p1, *k1, p5, k1, p1; repeat from * to last st, k1.

Row 7: K3, *p1, k3; repeat from * to last 4 sts, p1, k3.

Row 8: K1, p3, *k1, p1, k1, p5; repeat from * to last 7 sts, k1, p1, k1, p3, k1.

Repeat Rows 1–8 for pattern.

RIGHT SLANTING RIB

(multiple of 4 sts; 4-row repeat)

Row 1 (RS): *P2, k2; repeat from * to end.

Row 2: K1, *p2, k2; repeat from * to last 3 sts, p2, k1.

Row 3: *K2, p2; repeat from * to end.

Row 4: P1, *k2, p2; repeat from * to last 3 sts, k2, p1.

Repeat Rows 1–4 for pattern.

TRIANGLES B

(multiple of 12 sts + 1; 11-row pattern)

Row 1 (RS): P1, *k11, p1; repeat from * to end.

Row 2: K2, *p9, k3; repeat from * to last 11 sts, p9, k2.

Row 3: P2, *k9, p3; repeat from * to last 11 sts, k9, p2.

Row 4: K3, *p7, k5; repeat from * to last 10 sts, p7, k3.

Row 5: P3, *k7, p5; repeat from * to last 10 sts, k7, p3.

Row 6: K4, *p5, k7; repeat from * to last 9 sts, p5, k4.

Row 7: P4, *k5, p7; repeat from * to last 9 sts, k5, p4.

Row 8: K5, *p3, k9; repeat from * to last 8 sts, p3, k5.

Row 9: P5, *k3, p9; repeat from * to last 8 sts, k3, p5.

Row 10: K6, *p1, k11; repeat from * to * until last 7 sts, p1, k6.

Row 11: P6, *k1, p11; repeat from * to * until last 7 sts, k1, p6.

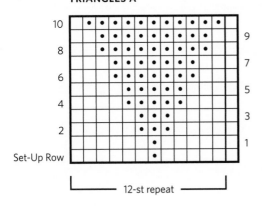

TRIANGLES A

12-st repeat

Set-Up Row

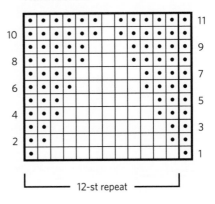

TRIANGLES B

12-st repeat

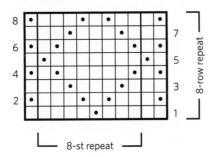

DIAMONDS

8-st repeat

8-row repeat

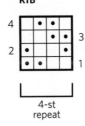

LEFT-SLANTING RIB

4-st repeat

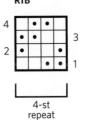

RIGHT-SLANTING RIB

4-st repeat

☐ Knit on RS, purl on WS.

▣ Purl on RS, knit on WS.

BLANKET

CO 85 (169) sts.

Knit 4 rows.

Work Set-Up Row, then Rows 1–10 of Triangles A.

Decrease Row: P2tog, purl to end—84 (168) sts remain.

Knit 1 row.

Work Rows 1–4 of Left Slanting Rib 3 times.

Purl 1 row.

Knit 2 rows.

Purl 2 rows.

Knit 2 rows.

Purl 1 row.

Knit 1 row.

Purl 1 row.

Eyelet Row (RS): K2, *k2tog, yo, k2; repeat from * to last 2 sts, k2.

Purl 1 row.

Knit 1 row.

Purl 2 rows.

Knit 1 row, decrease (increase) 1 (3) st(s) evenly across—83 (171) sts.

Work Rows 1–8 of Diamonds seven (14) times, then work Row 1 once more.

Knit 1 row, increasing 1 st on first row—84 (172) sts.

Purl 1 row.

Knit 1 row.

Purl 1 row.

Eyelet Row (RS): K2, *k2tog, yo, k2; repeat from * to last 2 sts, k2.

Purl 1 row.

Knit 1 row.

Purl 2 rows.

Knit 2 rows.

Purl 2 rows.

Knit 1 row.

Work Rows 1–4 of Right Slanting Rib 3 times.

Purl 1 row.

Knit 1 row, increase (decrease) 1 (3) st(s) evenly across—85 (169) sts.

Work Rows 1–11 of Triangles B.

Knit 5 rows.

BO all sts knitwise.

FINISHING

Block as desired.

Edging

With RS facing, beginning at one corner, pick up and knit approximately 110 (152) sts along long edge, picking up approximately 3 sts for every 4 rows.

Note: *Exact st count is not essential.*

Knit 7 rows. BO all sts knitwise.

Repeat for opposite edge.

Fringe

Find a small but sturdy, unbendable object that is approximately 1" (2.5 cm) longer than the finished length you want for your fringe. The finished fringe on the blanket shown measures approximately 2½" (6.5 cm) long, and I used a square wooden coaster. Wrap yarn around the object to create a bundle of strands, then cut the yarn at one end to release all the loops as single strands. Holding desired number of strands together, fold them in half, and using a crochet hook inserted into the edge of the blanket from back to front, draw the folded end through the edge and pull the loose end of the strands through the loop, then tighten the loop. Place a fringe at each corner of one short edge, then place the remaining fringes spaced approximately 1½" (4 cm) apart.

Steam the fringe lightly to straighten out any kinks and trim ends even.

NEW SHOOTS

SLIDE THE FIRST STITCH, WRAP, and repeat; the project grows and we grow with it—a climb and an expansion that reflects the deliberate but intentional movements of ivy and bougainvillea. I once watched a time-lapse video of pothos rotating throughout the day, seeking a foothold to climb upward. In the same way, our yarn and our fingers move in search of the next stitch, the yarn over, down-and-up-again, through-the-loop ritual of making fabric in thin air.

There is a magic, a meditative mood that we reach when we give our moments over to making. Depending on the project, I have found myself absorbed for hours that feel like minutes, or for a precious, dedicated half hour that feels like an infinite afternoon. The incantation of a stitch pattern emerges through quiet, mental repetition. The resulting fabric grows and reaches out from my hands, whirring instruments of my casting fingers bringing it into being.

Light in all forms brings life to delicate, planted seeds, and it also brings life and presence into the practice of making—morning sunlight, a moment stolen beside the steaming coffee cup in the early quiet; golden afternoon light spilling in from every window that slowly fades and is replaced by the flickering glow of a candle and warm illumination of a yellowed lampshade. What we make is the culmination of a seed planted in our minds. Our projects, for those who wear them, are like herbal remedies.

We gather these moments, this light, these finished objects around us in the same way that we gather bundles of fresh wildflowers, knowing that they cannot last forever and will fade with time, but enjoying every moment they are here with us.

summer solstice

SEASONAL KNITTERS

EARLY SUMMER IS SUCH A magical time of year. Spring has just finished her showy displays and everything begins to settle into a droning laziness. Sunlight moves in dappled pools beneath trees and beams brightly through open windows, announcing each day with excitement and vigor. The heady scent of flowers in bloom drifts through the air—a fragrant cocktail of roses, honeysuckle, jasmine, and gardenia.

There is a freedom to early summertime. This season invites us to get up, to get out and go, but also to stretch, to rest, and to observe. Weekend mornings offer us the promise of a quiet, serene moment before the heat of the day rises. These are some of my favorite mornings: moments stolen on the back patio, watching bees pick their way through the garden, listening to the ecstatic trill of birdsong.

I believe it's fair to characterize myself as a serious knitter. I am deeply passionate about this craft, and I always seem to have a sweater (or three) on the needles, but lately I find that my summers are slowing down, and my knitting has become more seasonal. It was not long ago that I frowned on seasonal knitters, somehow believing that they were less passionate or dedicated, but now I see the wisdom in letting go and embracing what is happening now.

Seasonal knitting isn't about entirely giving up on your craft in the warmer months. Rather, it's a moment of rest. Whenever I've had time away from my knitting, I feel invigorated to cast on something new. I find myself longing to return to a project, any project. A few stolen rounds on a sock in the late afternoon feel like a great accomplishment after a long day at the farmer's market or a hot day at the swimming pool. My knitting in these times becomes a calming, primarily indoor activity.

A rainy weekend spent knitting feels like the most luxurious of indulgences. In the South, we get rushing, wild storms that pour rain for hours at a time and then disappear, leaving only steaming cement and petrichor. On many summer evenings, rolling thunder and lightning take out power lines, plunging communities into sudden darkness. As a knitter, I try to make the most of evenings when electronics are temporarily unavailable; I look for the joy in lighting a bevy of candles and knitting in the soft glow until the hum of appliances is restored.

Rainy days become almost a treat: a break from the heat and the outside means a longer resting moment.

Allowing ourselves room to explore pursuits besides our knitting in other seasons also increases the fondness with which we return to needles and wool. The crispness of cotton and linen woven fabrics seems to be a delightful match for summer, and I love the low-commitment action of cutting pieces for a garment or stitching some quilt blocks in a single afternoon. Knitting can be a long-term commitment, even for the smallest projects, and sewing allows for a bit of flightiness and drift where it's needed. We must carry the inspiration that late spring and early summer provide with us into the cooler months, so spend time gathering it with your senses as much as possible, memorizing the colors, scents, and textures you experience throughout the season.

Summer is swatching and planning season. Embrace the desire to flutter from one yarn to another like a butterfly, swatching in various stitches and making notes, paging through pattern books and magazines in search of a project you'll cast on later in the year. The abundance of short bursts of time makes this season ideal for these sketches in yarn, and you'll be all the more grateful that you planned ahead when you're ready to cast on come autumn. Let the abundant color and texture of the natural world around you create an imprint from your spending time in it, and then carry that into your craft for the rest of the year.

slinky blends

Feeling the heat and eager to try some new fibers that are friendly to hot climates? Add enough of these silky fibers, and even a wool-blend yarn becomes tolerable in hot hands.

COTTON

Cool and smooth, spun cotton creates beautiful fabrics but in pure form can be challenging for new knitters, as 100 percent cotton yarns have no elasticity or give, which can make the stitches tight and difficult to manipulate. I prefer cotton in a blend with a softer animal fiber, like Merino wool or alpaca, but there are some very nice 100 percent cotton yarns on the market for those who want to try them.

The cultivation of cotton, like that of numerous other widely produced plants, has been under examination in recent years for its massive water requirements. There are many farmers and biologists working to develop more eco-friendly cottons, since cotton is one of the world's most commonly grown crops. Cleaner Cotton utilizes biofarming practices (like predator insects instead of pesticides) that eliminate the need for eleven of the most toxic chemicals used in conventional cotton production.

Scientist Sally Fox has also done remarkable things with cotton through her Foxfibre cotton breeding program. Sally seeks to create a premium cotton product that doesn't require a dye house, growing cottons that have naturally colored bolls in warm browns, earthy greens, and soft reds that intensify rather than fade with multiple washings.

SILK

The only monofilament (single-strand) natural fiber, silk adds shine to any blend, and the many types of silk create fabrics perfect for a variety of weather conditions. Silk fabric is thermoregulating, meaning that it adjusts to your body temperature. This makes silk a warm layer beneath sweaters, and a cool layer in the summer heat. I love silk blended with cotton, linen, or wool, but tend not to appreciate the squeakiness of knitting with 100 percent silk fibers. Silk is a wonderful material to pair with open lace stitches, as the fiber is very strong and reinforces the delicate structures.

If you love silk but find yourself concerned about the treatment of the caterpillars (who are typically exterminated in the production of traditional, reeled silk), I recommend learning more about the work of Cheryl Kolander, who is creating a caterpillar-friendly silk in the United States through her brand, Aurora Silk. I first learned about her through an interview on the *YarnStories* podcast with Miram Felton, and find her passion for these tiny creatures enchanting. One warning: If you have the room, you may find yourself hoping to raise silk caterpillars after listening!

LINEN

First cultivated by humans in Syria nine thousand years ago, flax is an exceptional plant that is the source of one of my favorite fibers and fabrics: linen. I most love to wear linen in the form of woven fabrics, not knitted ones, but this fiber's recent popularity has begun to spread to yarns in the form of 100 percent linen and linen blends. Purl Soho's Linen Quill, a blend of wool, alpaca, and linen, hits all the sweet spots for me in a blended, fingering-weight yarn with slight heathering. If you're wanting to try a 100 percent linen yarn, I recommend Shibui Knits' Reed.

While the production of linen has almost exclusively moved outside North America, there are efforts to bring the growth and processing of this fiber back, most notably by TapRoot Fibre Lab in Nova Scotia and Fibrevolution in the Willamette Valley, Oregon.

KNITTING IN THE HEAT

Occasionally we get one of those truly hot, miserable days. The air-conditioning seems almost sticky; rooms begin to feel a bit too close; the air, recirculated one too many times, smells stale and thin.

Luckily, being from a region where the temperature can remain well over 80°F (27°C) into October has given me time to develop some tricks for knitting in the heat.

KNIT SMALLER, QUICKLY FINISHED PROJECTS

My go-to summer knitting project is a pair of socks. Sock yarns are typically very smooth, and because they're lightweight they don't create thick fabrics your fingers have to manipulate. The resulting item is also small and doesn't feel heavy in your lap. Not into socks? Try projects that have small, modular parts you can knit one at a time. From household decorations to granny squares, there are tons of options in this category to choose from.

USE UP YOUR SUPERWASH STASH

While I have stopped purchasing superwash wools, I still have a considerable number of them lingering in my stash. The colors are so beautiful, I cannot part with them, so they will slowly be chosen, one by one, to become projects perfectly suited to them. A summer project in superwash means that you get to work with wool that is less likely to stick to your hands! Because superwash wools are designed to reduce friction and felting, they'll also ignore humidity, heat, and slightly damp skin.

SEEK OUT SLINKY FIBERS

For yarns that won't retain heat while you work with them, look for ones that have a high percentage of plant fibers or silk. Cotton, linen, hemp, silk, ramie, and bamboo are all great alternatives; opt for sleek fiber blends over fuzzy ones.

GO LIGHTWEIGHT

Smooth, lace-weight yarns worked up into intricate patterns can be the perfect companions for a hot day. Choose a project as complex as you want, but mark your chart so you know when you've completed a section and it's okay to break away. By doing so, you've assigned yourself little amounts of knitting you'll feel good about completing. It's easier to reward yourself with little bits of knitting throughout a hot day than to dig into a six-hour marathon project.

KEEP A COOL DRINK NEARBY

I'm not telling you this just to keep you hydrated, although that's certainly important. Holding a cold drink in your hands, and drinking liquids lower in temperature than you are, cools you down and make it easier to knit. Who doesn't love a cold glass of lemonade, sweet tea, or something a bit stronger on the porch in the afternoon?

REASSIGN YOUR EVENING ACTIVITIES

If you find that none of these tips are helping keep you cool enough to sit and knit, consider making evening your knitting time. Rearrange the furniture for this purpose, if necessary, positioning yourself near a fan, under a lamp with good light, and at a table where you can set your pattern and notions, and you'll be good to go!

KNITTING TRIPS

IN MY EARLY KNITTING YEARS, I never gave much thought to the fact that I didn't know many other knitters. My mother and younger sister were both fairly artistic and crafty, and so I was always surrounded by makers, although none of us were making the same things. My high school was a magnet school dedicated to inspiring and encouraging pursuit of the arts in teenagers. I dabbled in photography, plaster casting, clay sculpting, drawing, and painting. Knitting wasn't something I brought into my social life until the internet became a place to connect with other knitters. Paired with the rise of Ravelry, my knitting passions grew only more persistent and ambitious. I spent hours each evening in the forums, chatting with other knitters about projects they'd begun in similar yarns, or about colors they loved and wanted to work with. I learned new techniques and skills, and honed my ability to read patterns, which I printed out and slid into page protectors and began collecting in binders.

Meanwhile, I started to teach my friends how to knit, with a very low success rate. Many would never complete their first project. Then there were those who in their knitting burned the candle at both ends, quickly working through pattern after pattern until they suddenly hit a period of complete burnout and had no desire to pick up yarn or needles again. I was slowly cultivating a group of knitting friends online, but had very few in person.

I heard about a knitting club at my college, and went, only to find that everyone there had yet to move beyond the garter stitch, and none had been following the trends in knitting magazines or online. I longed for people to talk to about the nuances of Merino wool versus Bluefaced Leicester, about whether they preferred wooden or metal needles, and about how to deal with the tiny holes in my heels I kept getting while attempting to knit socks. Without a car, I was unable to attend knit nights hosted by the yarn shop on the other side of town, and so, as a knitter, I was an island, adrift in the sea of the internet each night and solitary by day.

My mother took pity on me and coordinated our first knitting trip together, to Stitches Midwest, just outside Chicago, in the summer, before I returned to school. I had no idea what awaited me at this event. We hadn't signed up to take any classes; we simply intended to visit the marketplace and see what yarns might be offered. We drove six hours and were in line early for the opening of the market. What was in store was more yarn than I had ever seen, and more knitters in a single place than I had ever dreamed. The crowd was a colorful array of plumage that I could identify by pattern and texture: It was my first time seeing the phenomenon of a "viral" pattern, a roomful of people wearing the same thing, each knit with a different yarn. I returned home invigorated and renewed.

Eventually, I was able to meet up with one of my first online knitting friends, Mary Catherine, in person. I was visiting Lexington, Kentucky, for a short stint, and she suggested we connect and visit some of the city's stores. I had never considered yarn tourism before, and eagerly made the date. Mary Catherine is bright-eyed and energetic, and we quickly translated our online friendship into a real-life one. We dug through yarn bins together and chose treasures to take home, then knit for a few hours in a café. The afternoon stuck with me long after we parted ways, and I realized that I had made a key error in my knitting trajectory: I had forgotten the joy and excitement of experiencing my craft in the company of others.

Making something with our hands using traditional needlework media—knitting, crochet, quilting, embroidery, needlepoint—is easy enough to do alone. None of the steps that I follow to knit a sock or a sweater, crochet an afghan, or sew a quilt require that I have another person present. The solitary nature of making is perhaps one of the reasons the methods and techniques have survived so long: Only one person is required to "carry on" the tradition of making, or to pass it along to someone else. Although it's entirely possible to keep your crafting to yourself, people who make textiles—traditionally, women—have historically preferred to make in groups, too. There is something about getting people together in the same space, to make different things using the same technique, that is special and encouraging.

Through gathering, we are able to learn new skills from one another or see different fabrics and projects in a new light. We can share reviews of the latest projects, patterns, and books, and mull over ideas. Only other, knitters can understand our excitement at a freshly finished garment, or the thrill of a new yarn acquisition. Isolation from this community deprives us of something integral to the craft: the exchange of ideas among peers. While the internet has provided a wonderful space for communication among knitters, it hasn't superseded something that I have found is a valuable part of each year: the knitting trip.

A knitting trip is a planned vacation, for yourself or a group, that takes you to a place where other knitters will also be in attendance. This can be a formal affair, like the New England Fiber Arts Summit, where there is a central location, classes and workshops, and a set number of attendees. If you're a solo traveler, organized events will be the best option for you to make connections starting out—you'll meet people in your classes and connect with them as you learn, eat, and relax together.

Planned knitting trips with friends are also necessary getaways that rejuvenate our excitement for this craft. Consider pulling together your knitting night group or working with your local yarn shop to assemble groups for the annual yarn crawl in your city, when you and several other knitters will carpool from shop to shop to see what each offers. When my mother and I ran our shop (The Sheep's Stockings) out of Marshalltown, Iowa, we loved the annual yarn crawl season and delighted in one particular group, which rented a seven-passenger van for the occasion. One woman's husband served as the designated non-knitting driver, so that the attendees could work on projects during the drive.

Traveling farther afield with other knitters is equally rewarding. Seeing a new place through the eyes of someone who is also passionate about fiber—and can talk to you about it along the way—is an amazing experience. I have the good fortune to be able to travel for each issue of *By Hand*, a knitting serial for which I am production editor. Andrea Hungerford, the author of these issues (each focused on a different city or region) and the creative mind behind them, has blessed me with the gift of travel for the past year, taking me along with her to interview makers in Asheville, Montana, New Hampshire, Portland, Seattle, Vermont, and other making communities. During these trips, we allow for plenty of knitting down time and visits to yarn and fabric stores. These detours would be tiresome for non-knitters, but are essential to our experience. After we leave each shop, we spend time discussing what we loved about the selection and atmosphere, and compare it to our favorite shops back home.

You don't need to travel far afield to get your knitting trip fix. Gather a few of your closest knitting friends and together choose a place to meet up and rest for a few days. Rent a cabin or a cozy apartment in a city you'd love to explore (check out the yarn shops online before you go), and get away for a few days with some like-minded folk who love to make as you do. Fill your mornings and evenings with time spent knitting, uninterrupted, and talk one another through the stresses and successes of your lives. This time connecting with other knitters is to be cherished, and you'll carry it home, to remember long after your knitting trip ends.

packing knitting for a trip

Packing is hard enough, honestly, without the added burden of being a knitter. Other people, I suppose, pack what they need for a trip, knowing that they will need exactly this many shirts, and this many socks, and this many pairs of underwear for the number of days they will be gone. They know that they might need to pack some extra hair conditioner, in case the hotel's offering is a bit sad, or that they need to bring a pillow from home for maximum comfort.

Knitters have no such guidelines to follow. It can be assumed that you, as a knitter, may need a project to work on at any time, in any situation, and therefore you must plan your travel knitting carefully so that you will never be without knitting in a moment of need.

First, there is the knitting that you pack in your most accessible bag. Whether this knitting goes into your backpack, tote, purse, or carry-on is up to you, but it's going to need to be lightweight and simple to follow on the go, and have very few notions needs. I typically take a scarf, socks, hat, or a single sweater sleeve designed to be worked separately from the body. Make sure your pattern instructions are in the same bag and, in the United States, that any scissors you need are TSA-approved (under 1" [2.5 cm] in blade length; other countries may have different requirements).

Next, you'll want to find a project to put into your suitcase—something entirely different and therefore infinitely more interesting than the pattern you're taking along for knitting en route. Depending on how much space you have in your bag and how long you'll be gone, consider taking a knit for each mood that might strike you. If you're a sweater knitter, bring along an extra hank in case you speed through the knitting and have to wind and add a new skein on the fly. If you're a scarf or shawl knitter, pack something ready to cast on and make sure to include plenty of stitch markers or the other notions you need. There is nothing worse than arriving at your destination and discovering that you've packed only one of the two needle sizes you require, or that you've run out of yarn the first few days into a project.

For long vacations with lots of down time, consider casting on something new that has been on your list for some time. I find that vacations pair very nicely with a dedicated, new project, and it answers the requirement that you get away from anything you already have developing at home. You're also more likely to give your full attention to a new project—and to be less swayed by any yarn temptations you encounter while visiting a new place!

Resist the temptation to throw a third or even fourth project into your bag, as it's very unlikely you'll get anything done on it. I never accomplish as much knitting as I would like when traveling, and there needs to be some room in the suitcase for clothing, too.

vacation yarns

As we go through the world as slower knitters, more conscientious and aware of our buying habits and knitting habits, we must also consider the value of the special stash acquisition known as vacation yarn. These yarns, bought while visiting somewhere far away from home, are purchases we make to remind us of the places we've been and what we discovered there.

Some of my most memorable knits have resulted from visiting new places and seeking out local yarn shops and fiber producers. I have a simple raglan sweater, creamy white in color, with pastel dots of confetti speckling, courtesy of a visit to Asheville, North Carolina. My first trip to Harrisville Designs, in New Hampshire, saw me arrive home with a sweater quantity of the golden colorway Foliage in their Shetland—which later became the sweater for the autumn section of this book. Many yarns I pick up on trips still have yet to communicate what they wish to become, like: some sock yarns from Montreal by way of Portland, Oregon, or the hot pink skein I picked up on a cloudy afternoon in New York City. How is it that we buy only yarn that dares us to dream while our judgment is confused by the romance of a spectacular location?

Is the yarn exclusive to this place? If the yarn is one that is also available close to home (perhaps from your local yarn shop), avoid buying it on vacation and instead spend the time you're away mulling over the ideas you have for projects. I would always rather support local businesses, which keeps the money in my own community and benefits the roads I drive on and the areas I frequent. Consider this: by purchasing a product your home shop sells while you are visiting a different locale, you are effectively choosing not to patronize your local yarn store. If the shop where you're vacationing has colors that your shop at home doesn't carry, consider placing a call and asking if your local store can special order it for you before pulling the trigger on a big purchase out of town.

If the yarn is exclusive—say, a farm yarn or a truly local yarn—come up with at least two ideas for items you'd like to make with it, and buy enough for your project in a single go, with a little wiggle room in case you change your mind. I have brought home three or four skeins from a shop, thinking that I will make a shawl, only to realize later that I should have purchased six or seven for a sweater.

Keep an eye on your buying patterns, too! I have a particular fondness for certain colors, and found upon sorting my stash last season that I had abundant representation in the greeny-yellow category, but hardly any of the comfortable neutrals I was craving to wear. Likewise, I have purchased enough single skeins of worsted-weight yarn to last me through about fifty hats—but I rarely wear hats, so the skeins must wait patiently until the mood strikes me and I cast on a hat. By identifying patterns we follow, we can avoid front-loading our stash with too much of the same, and can keep each purchase we make special and unique.

If you simply must bring home a souvenir from a delightful place you're visiting, look beyond the yarn to notions or limited-edition items the shop might carry. Some shops have exclusive deals with notions makers that allow them to have special colorways or offerings that other vendors may not. I have been known to pick up a project bag to remind me of my travels when the yarns aren't thrilling me. Items like buttons, tea, local candy, or greeting cards also make wonderful souvenirs (and don't take up as much space in your suitcase as wool!).

an argument for socks

There is a point of demarcation in the life cycle of any knitter. When we begin, we are eager to try anything and everything we are able to get our hands on, knitting hats and scarves, mittens and cowls, working with yarn of every type, color, and texture. At some point, a knitter might try to make a sweater for the first time and discover a love for garments in addition to every other knitting possibility. The fork in the road of our knitting journey often comes when we begin our first pair of socks. There are so many factors that affect the success of this first pair that the initial experience is all but critical in setting knitters up for a lifetime of sock knitting, or apathetic disdain for the process.

By knitting a first sock on worsted-weight yarn, students learn nothing about the fit and nuances of an ultratight-gauge fabric's strength and hand. They are working with a yarn never intended for socks, to create objects a bit too thick and bulky to be comfortably worn—leading many to believe, when they feel the purl ridges on their soles the first time they wear them, that handknit socks are uncomfortable. While taking things to a larger scale may seem like a good approach, in reality socks are small—so why not learn them at the correct scale?

If they're not already comfortable working with multiple needles on small circumferences, balancing a fiddly cast-on and the stress of dropping a needle will turn some crafters away from making footwear. In addition, the fine gauge of sock yarn can be daunting to those who have worked only in larger needle sizes. These obstacles are easily surmounted, of course, given the many ways there are to knit socks. While one sock knitter will excel on double points, another will give up and never try an alternative method, although a lesson in Magic Loop might have provided the courage to continue!

Lastly, fit is an indicator of success for any inaugural pair of socks, and is one of the most difficult elements for first-time sock knitters to attain. Since they have never attempted a pair of socks before, their first pairs are almost destined to be far from perfect. The heel might be a bit too wide, or the foot too loose. Perhaps the cast-on round is so tight that it is a struggle to get the sock on, or the Kitchener stitch grafting at the toe is a bit lumpy and wonky because it's a first attempt. Working directly from a sock pattern without measuring your own leg, foot, and heel against the instructions can yield unexpected results, especially in "fancy" socks with lace and cables. Even the most level-headed, experienced knitters get frustrated by socks that simply don't fit properly.

On the opposite path is the crafter destined to fall in love with socks. Where others see skinny yarns and tiny needles, she sees an endless opportunity to play with color in her wardrobe. Hidden away safely inside a pair of boots, socks can be made with wild and unexpected yarns, in vibrant colors or subdued, everyday tones. There is no need to worry about the socks being unseen—that is the goal. Socks are a secret, selfish project that brings happiness to the maker and wearer.

The sock knitter sees each pair as a singular opportunity to further hone his craft. After the first, wonky pair, tiny changes may be made: a new heel to try, a new cast-on, or a chance to work from the toe up, rather than the cuff down. Each sock is a tiny commitment to a new technique and a tweak of the previous attempt. While all socks may not be loved equally, no sock is useless: Into the drawer the pair goes, to be worn on laundry day, or lent to a chilly friend, or gifted to someone they fit better. Socks are small, low-commitment projects perfect for experimentation.

After you have knitted the first few pairs, you begin to discover the modifications most

suited to your foot's shape, and develop preferences for heel types, gauge, and method. It doesn't take long for each sock knitter to develop their own go-to pattern: a riff on the simple Stockinette sock, with all the edits needed to make fit and shape ideal for your own foot. These couture knits are easy to carry with you, rendering them the perfect travel project.

The reward of a pair of finished socks can't be beat. While it's not quite as thrilling as binding off a sweater, there is far less finishing to be done. With the last bind-off on the cuff or last stitch of the toe complete, sock knitters soon discover something akin to the potato-chip effect: You can never make just one! I have finished sets of socks and slipped them on the very same evening, simply tucking the ends into the leg in order to admire and appreciate them immediately. No blocking is required; your foot will do the work for you.

Caring for socks is easy, too. Superwash wools have given many sock knitters the illusion that all socks should be machine-washed, but I find that even the best-quality superwash looks faded and worn when thrown in with the week's wash. I handwash all my socks now, and it has become a bit of a weekly ritual in the fall and winter, and never feels like a chore. A sink filled with colorful, wooly socks is a joyous sight, and it's possible to wash all your socks at the same time, then hang them to dry, creating cheery garlands.

Above all, wearing handknit socks is a most luxurious experience. Slipping a pair of truly warm, woolen socks over chilly feet is the height of indulgence. No cotton, store-bought sock can compare to a handknit sock in squishy heft, or in the coziness it brings to our ankles and toes. While others may scoff at the idea of making something so plebian by hand, when they are readily available at any shop, you will know that they are wrong. Having this secret something all your own in a world of other knitters and people who can't quite get it—that is the argument for socks.

SOCK KNITTER'S KIT

SOCK-SUITABLE NEEDLES

Whether you're seeking to knit your socks in the round, on double points, or two at a time, your needle choices matter. Try knitting socks on various needle types and styles until you find the ones you love most. My ideal sock needles have a pointy tip, and I have different preferences for different knitting styles. I prefer my double points to be made from a strong material like steel or carbon fiber. For circulars, I like the speed of nickel plating, or the hand of wooden needles, and a superflexible cord is always a must.

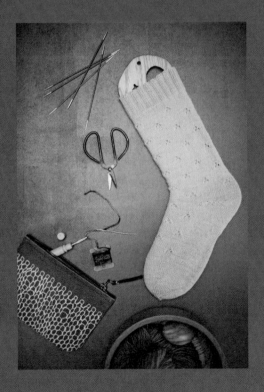

NOTIONS POUCH

A notions pouch small enough to fit into my sock project bag is a must! With a zipper, this pouch contains all the sundries I need to start and finish a pair on the go.

SCISSORS

A small pair of scissors is always handy when knitting socks, especially if you want to weave in your ends and wear the socks right away after finishing.

BENT-TIP TAPESTRY NEEDLE

Tapestry needles come in both straight or bent-tip varieties, but I strongly prefer the bent-tip needle for Kitchener stitch and weaving in ends accurately.

DARNING EGG OR MUSHROOM

I love collecting vintage darning eggs and mushrooms wherever I can find them, but I never mind picking up a pretty one from a wood-turning craftsman offering them, either. I prefer heavier wooden objects to light ones (like a plastic Easter egg) as they feel a bit sturdier in the hand.

EMBROIDERY CARDS

Available in plastic, paper, and even wooden varieties, embroidery cards make excellent storage for a little bit of extra yarn you might need later to darn your socks. Handknit socks are beautiful, durable things, but at some point they'll need some tender, loving care. Prepare accordingly by having some of the same yarn on hand to make near-invisible darns.

sock knitting methods

There are so many ways to cast on and knit socks! Finding enjoyment in the process is simply a matter of finding the right order of operations and method for your process and knitting style. I recommend trying as many methods as possible before settling on a favorite.

NEEDLE STYLES

Double Points: Double-pointed needles are many knitters' top choice for working small circumferences in the round. If you have solved the problem of laddering (uneven tension when switching from one needle to another), these are also a wonderfully portable and flexible way to knit socks, especially when it comes to turning the heel or trying the socks on as you go. (Add another needle and there is enough room to try on—stick with three during the heel to keep the instep stitches stable.) These are available in wood, various metals, carbon fiber, plastic, and even glass—choose your material based on how frequently you sit on your project or stuff it into other bags.

Circulars: You can use a very small single circular needle to knit a single 9" (23 cm) or larger sock, or venture into the Magic Loop or TAAT methods of circular setup. It is important that circulars have near-seamless joins at these small gauges and that the cord is long enough and flexible enough to use for the TAAT or Magic Loop methods.

METHOD

TAAT (Two at a Time)/Magic Loop: Using a single long circular or two circular needles, this method makes two socks at the same time in an attempt to solve "second sock syndrome." These socks are generally cast on at the same time and the first few rounds—whether top down or toe up—are especially fiddly, but some knitters consider this an even exchange for being done with both socks simultaneously. Pay close attention to your pattern. If your pattern features reflected elements (like cables or lace), it can be easy to get lost with all the changing about!

ORDER OF OPERATIONS

Top Down/Cuff Down: This method of sock construction begins with a very stretchy cast-on at the cuff and moves through the leg, heel, and foot of the sock before ending at the toe. Some methods like the Afterthought Heel may end with the heel worked last. My favorite cast-on methods for top-down socks include Jeny's Super Stretchy Cast-on and the German Long-Tail Cast-on (see Special Techniques, page 188). I don't recommend a standard Long-Tail or Knitted Cast-on as they are not quite stretchy enough for most socks. When knitting top down, you'll need to have a tapestry needle on hand when finishing to graft your toes using the Kitchener stitch.

Toe Up: This method of sock construction begins at the toe, using a tight cast-on and fewer stitches, then works through the foot, heel, and leg of the sock before ending with a stretchy bind-off at the cuff. Cast-on methods for Toe-Up socks include the Figure 8 Cast-on and Turkish Cast-on. When knitting toe up, you'll need to bind off your cuff with an elastic edge. My favorite bind-off for toe-up socks is Jeny's Surprisingly Stretchy Bind-off.

Play around with different sock construction methods until you find the perfect fit for your knitting style. Experiment fearlessly with different heels, toes, cast-ons, and bind-offs to create a sock recipe that is uniquely yours!

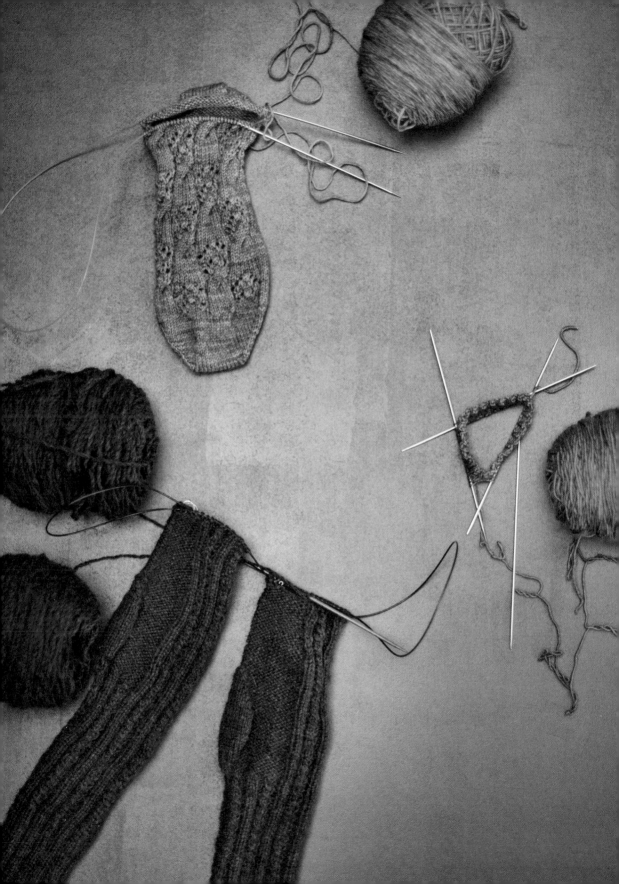

Kathryn Gail Socks

/ About the Yarn /

BEAVERSLIDE DRY GOODS MULE-SPUN YARN:
2-PLY SPORT/SOCK WEIGHT

In a world in which we're all trying to cut down on our plastic consumption, it can be difficult to find a sock yarn that is not superwash (which in most methods coats the yarn in a polymer) and doesn't include nylon (which is a synthetic, polymer fiber). Mohair is the natural nylon, with exceptional elasticity, stretch, and durability, and I predict we'll be seeing its inclusion in many more sock yarns as consumers make a slow but steady shift toward more sustainable materials.

This soft, woolen-spun sock yarn is milled along the backbone of North America by Beaverslide Dry Goods, a family-owned business that is based at the foot of the Rocky Mountains in northern Montana. There, Leanne Hayne and her family raise a flock of Merino sheep, crossbred with some Merinos that also carry Delaine genes for increased loftiness and lanolin. Beaverslide ships its yarn over the border to Canada for processing, at a mill that still operates equipment used in the late 1800s. The mill does a minimal amount of processing, so the wool is never exposed to massive heat or chemicals, and then the yarn is mule-spun with a Z-twist that allows each skein to fluff in the most delightful way.

While this 2-ply might seem a bit delicate in the skein, this structure teaches knitters much-needed patience; pull too hard, and your stitch may give way and break! If you're willing to slow down and take your time on the cast-on, though, the resulting lofty, squishable stitches will have you wishing for weather chilly enough to take advantage of these warm and cozy socks. The finished fabric is thin and light, and saving a little of your leftovers for darning is advised. A little stitching on my end, though, is a small price to pay for keeping microplastics out of our water systems, and supporting a beautifully made North American yarn.

SIZES

Note: See Notes on Fit for clarification on determining which size to work.

Foot Circumference: Narrow (Average, Wide)

To fit above-ankle circumferences 8 (9½, 12¼)" [20.5 (24, 31) cm]

To fit foot sizes Women's Small/Men's X-Small, Women's Medium/Men's Small, Women's Large/Men's Medium, Women's X-Large/Men's Large, Women's 2X-Large/Men's X-Large

To fit US shoe sizes Women's 5-6/Men's 4-5, Women's 7-8/Men's 6-7, Women's 9-10/Men's 8-9, Women's 11-12/Men's 10-11, Women's 13-14/Men's 12-13

FINISHED MEASUREMENTS

Sock Foot Length: 8½ (9, 9½, 10, 10½)" [21.5 (23, 24, 25.5, 26.5) cm]

Sock Foot Circumference: 6¼ (7½, 9¾)" [16 (19, 25) cm], unstretched

Note: Sock will stretch when worn to fit foot of circumferences 8 (9½, 12¼)" [20.5 (24, 31) cm].

NOTES ON FIT

For the best fit, you will base your sizing on two measurements: your above-ankle circumference (where your cuff is most likely to sag if not fit properly) and your foot length. You will cast on and work through the pattern according to stitch counts calculated from your chosen above-ankle circumference [Narrow (Average, Wide)]. When you reach the foot of the sock, the length to work the foot will be based on your chosen foot length or foot size (Women's Small/Men's X-Small, Women's Medium/Men's Small, Women's Large/Men's Medium, Women's X-Large/Men's Large, Women's 2X-Large/Men's X-Large) or shoe size (Women's 5-6/Men's 4-5, Women's 7-8/Men's 6-7, Women's 9-10/Men's 8-9, Women's 11-12/Men's 10-11, Women's 13-14/Men's 12-13).

These socks have some negative ease built in, so remember that the measurements under SIZES are the measurements when worn, not the measurements according to gauge or on the needles; the FINISHED MEASUREMENTS are when the completed sock is laid flat, unstretched. For reference, the stretched (on the foot) gauge is 22 stitches over 4" (10 cm).

YARN

Beaverslide Dry Goods Mule-Spun Yarn 2-Ply Sport/Sock Weight [80% Merino wool/20% fine kid mohair; 458 yards (419 meters)/4 ounces (113 grams)]: 1 skein Charcoal

ALTERNATIVE YARNS

Light sport-weight or heavy fingering-weight yarn in the amounts listed in the chart below.

(Canada) Julie Asselin Nomade (80% North American superwash Merino wool/20% nylon)

(Finland) Tukuwool Fingering (100% Finnish wool)

(UK) Blacker Mohair Blends 4-Ply (34% Hebridean wool/33% Manx wool/33% mohair)

If you are a knitter who pulls yarns very tight or who has a tendency to break woolen-spun strands, you can always substitute a thicker, fingering-weight handspun wool, or another plied yarn of your choice that allows you to get a nice, tight fabric at gauge.

NEEDLES

Size US 1½ (2.5 mm) needle(s) in your preferred style for working in the rnd

Change needle size if necessary to obtain correct gauge.

NOTIONS

Stitch markers; cable needle (optional)

GAUGE

28 sts and 36 rnds = 4" (10 cm) in St st, unstretched
Note: St gauge will stretch to approximately 22 sts = 4" (10 cm) when worn.

TO FIT FOOT LENGTH	TO FIT ABOVE-ANKLE CIRCUMFERENCE		
	Narrow [8" (20.5 cm)]	Average [9½" (24 cm)]	Wide [12¼" (31 cm)]
Women's Small/Men's X-Small [8½" (21.5 cm)]	195 yards (178 meters)	250 yards (229 meters)	345 yards (315 meters)
Women's Medium/Men's Small [9" (23) cm]	205 yards (187 meters)	255 yards (233 meters)	360 yards (329 meters)
Women's Large/Men's Medium [9½" (24 cm)]	210 yards (192 meters)	265 yards (242 meters)	365 yards (334 meters)
Women's X-Large/Men's Large [10" (25.5 cm)]	215 yards (197 meters)	270 yards (247 meters)	375 yards (343 meters)
Women's 2X-Large/Men's X-Large [10½" (26.5 cm)]	225 yards (206 meters)	280 yards (256 meters)	390 yards (357 meters)

SPECIAL ABBREVIATION

LT (Left Twist): Insert needle from back to front between first and second stitches and knit second stitch, then knit first stitch and slip both stitches from left needle together. To work using a cable needle, slip 1 stitch to cable needle and hold to front, k1, k1 from cable needle.

PATTERN NOTES

To simplify the process and finish both socks at once, I prefer to use the Magic Loop, Two-at-a-Time method (see Special Techniques, page 188); however, you can cast on using whatever method you choose. If you are using Magic Loop, I recommend watching a video on setting up socks using this method on YouTube or on my website.

With any sock, the most important first step is to calculate your gauge. For well-fitting socks, this is absolutely critical. Knit your swatch in the round on the same needle(s) and, using the same method for knitting in the round that you will use for your socks (so use Magic Loop if you are working either Magic Loop or TAAT). I am slowly transitioning to using only a handful of favorite sock yarns and needles so that I can avoid this step more often in the future, and encourage any dedicated sock knitter to do the same.

Jeny's Super Stretchy Cast-on (see Special Techniques, page 188) is my go-to for socks, since my lower calf is a bit wider than my ankle. I appreciate the extra stretch it provides, but it can be a bit tricky the first few times you attempt it, since it is a series of slipknots and they need to be made evenly throughout. Practice a bit with a sturdier yarn before casting on with the Beaverslide if this is a new technique for you, and don't be too discouraged if your actual CO attempt looks a bit messy—this will stretch and even out over time and wear. (If you choose to do a Magic Loop set-up and it's giving you trouble, it might be worth it to cast on your initial row onto DPNs, then change to Magic Loop after a few rnds.)

Additionally, there are some sweet little bonus techniques mixed into this sock that make them more comfortable to wear and add to the overall fit.

The "pocket heel" used in this pattern was first designed by Miriam Felton, a dear friend and extremely clever knitter. Miriam invented it while seeking an alternative heel for high instep feet—feet that have a wider measurement from the ankle bone to the top of the foot than from the ankle bone to the back of the heel. It is an increase heel without

a turn or any picked-up stitches that fits high instep heels nicely. If you have a high instep, or if your foot simply doesn't seem to fit well into a traditional flap heel or short-row heel, you may find that this heel is a wonderful alternative for you. It's very easy to get the gist of, too, so you can plug it into almost any pattern with ease. Miriam has graciously allowed me to print it here for you.

I have high arches as well as a high instep, so I like to add a little arch shaping to my sock to keep from having wiggle at the base of the heel. If you also find that you wear your heels out on the bottom of the foot (not against the back of the shoe), this modification may be helpful to you. The foot has the smooth side of Stockinette stitch turned inside for a "princess sole" that sensitive feet enjoy, and there is an option for hidden arch shaping in the foot section.

CUFF

Note: *The numbers given in each 3-number numerical sequence throughout the pattern correspond to the to-fit above-ankle circumferences Narrow (Average, Wide) (see SIZES). Due to the wide range of foot lengths, lengths will be given separately within the pattern according to to-fit foot lengths (see SIZES). Choose both the to-fit above-ankle circumference and to-fit foot length before beginning.*

Using Jeny's Super Stretchy Cast-on (see Special Techniques, page 188), CO 44 (52, 68) sts (see Pattern Notes). Divide sts as evenly as possible.

Rnd 1: *K2, p2; repeat from * to end.

Repeat Rnd 1 until piece measures 3½" (9 cm) from the beginning.

LEG

Rnd 1: *LT, p2, k2, p2; repeat from * to last 4 sts, LT, p2.

Note: *There is an LT column at the beginning and end of the rnd with a column of 2 purl sts between.*

Rnds 2 and 3: *K2, p2; repeat from * to end.

Repeat Rnds 1–3 until piece measures approximately 7" (18 cm) from the beginning, ending with Rnd 3.

Note: *If desired, you may lengthen the leg another 2" (5 cm) without compromising the fit around the calf; keep in mind that if you lengthen the leg, you may require additional yarn.*

POCKET HEEL

Rnd 1: *LT, p2, k2, p2; repeat from * to last 4 sts, LT, p1, pm for heel shaping, M1L, pm for heel shaping, p1—45 (53, 69) sts.

Rnd 2: P10 (12, 16), pm for beginning of instep, work as established over 22 (26, 34) sts, pm for end of instep, purl to next marker, sm, k1, sm, p1.

Increase Rnd: Purl to marker, sm, work to next marker, sm, purl to next marker, sm, M1R, knit to marker, M1L, sm, purl to end—2 sts increased.

Resting Rnd: Purl to marker, sm, work to next marker, sm, purl to next marker, sm, knit to marker, sm, purl to end.

Repeat the last 2 rnds 4 (5, 6) times—55 (65, 83) sts; 11 (13, 15) sts between heel-shaping markers.

Decrease Rnd: Purl to marker, sm, work to next marker, sm, purl to next marker, sm, ssk, knit to 2 sts before next marker, k2tog, sm, purl to end—2 sts decreased.

Work a Resting Rnd.

Repeat the last 2 rnds 4 (5, 6) times—44 (53, 69) sts remain; 1 st between heel markers.

Next Rnd: Purl to marker, sm, work to next marker, sm, purl to next marker, remove marker, ssp (removing marker), purl to end—44 (52, 68) sts remain; 22 (26, 34) sts each for instep and sole.

ARCH SHAPING (OPTIONAL)

Note: *This modification may be helpful to you if you have high arches or wear your heels out on the bottom of the foot (not against the back of the shoe). If you prefer not to work arch shaping, skip ahead to the FOOT section.*

Round 1: Purl to 2 sts before marker, ssp, sm, work to next marker, sm, p2tog, purl to end—2 sole sts decreased.

Rnd 2: Purl to marker, sm, work to next marker, sm, purl to end.

Repeat Rnds 1 and 2 based on your chosen foot length and foot size, as follows:

Women's Small/Men's X-Small and Women's Medium/Men's Small: Repeat Rnds 1 and 2 three more times—36 (44, 60) sts remain; 22 (26, 34) sts for instep and 14 (18, 26) sts for sole.

Women's Large/Men's Medium and Women's X-Large/Men's Large: Repeat Rnds 1 and 2 four more times—34 (42, 58) sts remain; 22 (26, 34) sts for instep and 12 (16, 24) sts for sole.

Women's 2X-Large/Men's X-Large: Repeat Rnds 1 and 2 five more times—32 (40, 46) sts remain; 22 (26, 34) sts for instep and 10 (14, 22) sts for sole.

FOOT

If you didn't add the optional arch shaping, work even to desired foot length, or until piece reaches the second knuckle of your big toe. You may use the number of rnds or lengths given below for each foot length or foot size, or customize the length as follows: The pocket heel will end almost immediately with the slight upturn of the heel on the bottom of the foot. Measure the distance from the point at which your foot becomes heel (the skin changes and gets a bit thicker when it's heel, if that helps you find the right spot) to the second knuckle of your big toe, then, continuing to work in rib pattern as established on instep sts and in reverse St st (purl every rnd) on sole sts, work even until piece measures that length from end of pocket heel.

Rnds/length from end of pocket heel to second knuckle of big toe:

Women's Small/Men's X-Small: 42 rnds; 4¾" (12 cm) long

Women's Medium/Men's Small: 50 rnds; 5½" (14 cm) long

Women's Large/Men's Medium: 54 rnds; 6" (15 cm) long

Women's X-Large/Men's Large: 58 rnds; 6½" (16.5 cm) long

Women's 2X-Large/Men's X-Large: 68 rnds; 7½" (19 cm) long

Change to St st (knit every rnd) across all sts; knit 1 rnd.

TOE (IF YOU DIDN'T WORK ARCH SHAPING)

Decrease Rnd: [Knit to 3 sts before marker, ssk, k1, sm, k1, k2tog] twice, knit to end—4 sts decreased.

Repeat Decrease Rnd every other rnd 6 (5, 3) more times, then every rnd 0 (3, 9) times—16 sts remain; 8 each for instep and sole.

TOE (IF YOU WORKED ARCH SHAPING)

Note: *You will first decrease the instep sts to match the sole sts, then work additional decreases to shape the toe.*

Decrease Rnd 1: Knit to marker, k2tog, knit to 2 sts before next marker, ssk, sm, knit to end—2 instep sts decreased.

Repeat Decrease Rnd 1 as follows:

Women's Small/Men's X-Small and Women's Medium/Men's Small: Repeat Decrease Rnd 1 every other rnd 3 (3, 2) more times, then every rnd 0 (0, 1) time(s)—28 (36, 52) sts remain; 14 (18, 26) sts each for instep and sole. Work 1 (1, 0) rnd(s) even.

Women's Large/Men's Medium and Women's X-Large/Men's Large: Repeat Decrease Rnd 1 every other rnd 4 (4, 2) more times, then every rnd 0 (0, 2) times—24 (32, 48) sts remain; 12 (16, 24) sts each for instep and sole. Work 1 (0, 0) rnd(s) even.

Women's 2X-Large/Men's X-Large: Repeat Decrease Rnd 1 every other rnd 5 (4, 2) more times, then every rnd 0 (1, 3) time(s)—20 (28, 44) sts remain; 10 (14, 22) sts each for instep and sole.

Decrease Rnd 2: [Knit to 3 sts before marker, ssk, k1, sm, k1, k2tog], knit to end—4 sts decreased.

Repeat Decrease Rnd 2 as follows:

Women's Small/Men's X-Small and Women's Medium/Men's Small: Repeat Decrease Rnd 2 every other rnd 1 (0, 0) more time(s), then every rnd 1 (4, 8) time(s)—16 sts remain; 8 sts each for instep and sole.

Women's Large/Men's Medium and Women's X-Large/Men's Large: Repeat Decrease Rnd 2 every rnd 1 (3, 7) more time(s)—16 sts remain; 8 sts each for instep and sole.

Women's 2X-Large/Men's X-Large: Repeat Decrease Rnd 2 every rnd 0 (2, 6) more times—16 sts remain; 8 sts each for instep and sole.

FINISHING

Using Kitchener stitch, graft toes together. No blocking is necessary; these socks will block out with wear.

MIDSUMMER GIFTING

ISN'T IT INTERESTING THAT MOST of our focus on gift knitting is concentrated on the Yuletide season, when there are so many other opportunities to gift those we love with beautiful knits? It does always seem that someone's birthday is around the corner, and every year I am touched that my family members and friends remember mine—a sentiment shared by many who have aged out of birthday parties and annual celebrations. A small knit can go a long way—herb sachets, a drawstring jewelry pouch with a single bright button, or even a set of felted coasters can be a lovely gift in no time at all.

Baby showers seem abundant in the spring and summer, and new babies can always use a wooly something for the upcoming winter. I once made a tiny set of Saartje's Bootees and a little hat for my sister to take to a baby shower, and the mother featured it months later in the newborn photoshoot!

When knitting for little ones, think outside your "standard" palette. Richly saturated tones make for exceptional photos that new parents love. Some of my favorite go-to colors for infants and toddlers include emerald green, cobalt blue, mustard yellow, and deep wine red.

For children four to eight years old, there are many lovely plush toy patterns available, some of which have full wardrobes of fantastic clothing to knit (and therefore set you up for the perfect present for every occasion for at least a few years!).

Some brides are returning to the tradition of the bridal shawl, and it's not uncommon to see a knitter working on delicate lace, sometimes adorned with beads, for an upcoming wedding gift. If you have a bride in your life, make sure you consult her before knitting something so personal; it would be easier for her to turn you down than to leave it off on her wedding day after you've made it!

I appreciate the magic of using your craft to create something beautiful for someone you love. I tend to make things in advance of determining their owners, to remove some of the stress, and instead, I stock up on baby sweaters, blankets, hats, and handwarmers, and wait for the right moment to wrap one up and send it along.

Wrapping gifts in the summer season can be a more casual affair than your holiday setup. With all the world in bloom, consider a tiny wildflower bouquet against a backdrop of simple brown paper or pastel tissue paper for a sweet, sentimental gift. Gray-and-white newsprint with a bundle of lichen-covered twigs and some bright green leaves give a deep, woodsy feel for adults, while a giant, exuberant sunflower is the perfect fit for a little girl's birthday party.

Sewn Notions Pouch

I love having the ability to go anywhere at a moment's notice, to grab my knitting bag and know that everything I need will be inside. I've only begun to make a habit of prepping each project bag I use when I begin a project, but it makes such a difference to the portability of my knitting that I daresay I'm addicted. When I choose a new pattern, I put a copy of the pattern, any needles I'll need (interchangeables are especially handy here), and a notions pouch into the project bag I'll be using for that work in progress. By identifying the notions I need before I begin, I never have to go hunting for the tapestry needle or pair of scissors when it's time to use them—I have them on hand.

A little zippered pouch is the perfect place to store these types of notions, and it's easy to sew. Not only do these pouches make wonderful additions to your own project bags, they're also fantastic ways to up the ante on your next swap packages or gifts for knitting friends. You'll need about a two-hour window to make one, but if you cut and prep at once, you could make ten or more at a time. Only the ability to sew straight lines on a sewing machine is needed.

Use almost any fabric you like! Quilting cottons, heavier cottons, waxed canvas, wool, corduroy, or medium- to home-decor-weight fabrics work beautifully for these pouches.

MATERIALS

One piece of fabric for the backing

An equal size piece of fabric for the lining

An equal-size piece of nonfusible home-decor-weight interfacing

A zipper the same length as the width of the pouch or longer

Ruler or quilting ruler

Quilting clips or pins

Scissors

Begin by attaching the zipper foot to your sewing machine. Most machines come with a zipper foot; if your machine doesn't have a zipper foot, you'll need to take a trip to your local sewing machine shop to buy one, or you can order one for most machines online. Without a zipper foot, this process will be much harder, and you could break a needle if you are using the wrong foot.

Layer all three fabrics together as a sandwich. The lining material needs to face down, the interfacing goes in the middle, and the backing should face up.

With the backing facing up, use quilting clips or pins to secure the zipper to your fabric. The zipper should be facing down, with the toothed edges toward the inside of the zipper as shown.

Using the zipper foot for your machine, sew a ¼" (6 mm) seam as close to the zipper teeth as possible without going over them with the needle or thread. Your zipper foot should help guide the fabric through and keep the zipper straight as you sew.

Flip the entire fabric sandwich so that the lining is facing you, with the zipper side you have already sewn on the top, and the still-loose zipper and fabric sandwich on the bottom.

Adjust your fabric sandwich layers so they are smooth and straight, and secure them to the zipper with quilting clips or pins. The zipper pull should be completely open for this step. Sew along this side as you did for the previous side.

Keeping the lining fabric facing you, press the sides of your pouch with an iron so that you have an equal amount of fabric on both the front and the back of your pouch. Close the zipper so you can get everything aligned properly.

The easiest way to do this is to make sure your zipper is positioned at the center of the pouch; just measure it from either side and make small adjustments to center it in the middle of what will become the top of your pouch. Or, if you prefer, shift it so the zipper has ½" (1.3 cm) of the fabric on one side for a different style option.

Sew a ¼" (6 mm) seam down the short length of the pouch on each side, sewing across the bottom of the zipper on one end and the top of the zipper on the other (making sure the zipper pull is to the inside of the seam). Your pouch is now fully enclosed; trim threads and clean up the inside.

Clip any excess zipper off the end. Now that your zipper is secured by the seams, it is safe to remove the length of zipper you won't be using.

Turn your pouch inside out—it's finished! Now you can put all your favorite notions inside and have them on the go.

FABRIC-WRAPPED GIFTS

Looking for a sweet way to wrap the gift of new yarn or a finished project for a friend? Furoshiki, the Japanese practice of fabric wrapping, provides inspiration for an easy and eco-friendly packaging option. All you'll need to create a beautiful bundle is a silk scarf and a handwritten note.

There are endless options for wrapping with fabric, but sometimes the simplest variation is my method of choice. For this pretty bundle of two skeins, you'll want a square silk scarf. Place your item in the center of the scarf and pick up two opposite corners of the scarf, letting them meet in the center over the item. Tie them together with a simple overhand knot. Bring the other two opposite corners to the center, and tie them together with a simple overhand knot, too. Now you're ready to gift. This style is known as the Four-Tie Wrap, or *Yotsu Musubi* in Japanese.

five wool breeds to try

When visiting a wool festival, it seems almost mandatory that you strive to discover something new to take home with you. Interacting with farmers, ranchers, and local producers gives knitters the opportunity to experience new fibers and textures that are similar to but different from what we use most frequently.

CORMO

No longer relegated to festival stalls, this bouncy Merino alternative seems to have exploded onto the commercial market as of late, showing up in a variety of delightful (and highly available) yarns. Cormo is technically a longer wool than Merino, but Cormo and Cormo-cross sheep have recently been producing wonderfully fine fleeces that are making their way to knitters in the form of bouncy, double- or triple-plied skeins.

Recommendations: Foxhill Farm is a favorite at the NY State Sheep and Wool Festival for its Cormo, but you can also find wonderful Cormo from Stone Wool or in Harrisville Designs' Nightshades line.

TARGHEE

Full of personality, this fiber is one of my favorites to spin and knit for almost anything. I've got Targhee-based sweaters, socks, and accessories, and this medium wool performs well in all applications. As a fiber, it feels crunchier than ultrasoft Merino, but not stiff or itchy.

Recommendations: Brooklyn Tweed's Shelter and Loft both use a Targhee-Columbia cross in a woolen-spun structure for maximum lightness, while Sincere Sheep's Bannock has a smoother structure that takes advantage of the density of this wool in a variety of soft, naturally dyed colors.

CHEVIOT

If you enjoy toothier wools like Corriedale and Shetland, Cheviot is a logical next step toward truly wooly wools. The spin on this yarn is essential, as is a quality fleece, but when properly sourced and spun Cheviot has a hardy feel that is not easily matched. In a skein, it feels dense and sturdy: reliable for nearly any project. The softer fibers seem to rise to the top of the knitted fabric, giving finished pieces with Cheviot a smooth look

and a lightly brushed feel, without the excessive pilling that often occurs with softer fibers.

Recommendations: It's quite difficult to find a Cheviot or 100 percent Cheviot yarn, but Whistlebare in Northumberland, in the United Kingdom, offers Cheviot blended with both Bluefaced Leicester and Perendale wools.

ROMNEY

It seems like Romney is enjoying a bit of a resurgence in the knitting world. Previously, this slinky longwool was used exclusively for industrial applications, carpeting, and tapestry weavings. Thanks to the revival of interest in heirloom wools, Romney has begun to appear in the yarn lines of many of my favorite companies. Certainly suited for outerwear, Romney has a shine and strength that is unparalleled by other fibers, and the finished fabrics look excellent even with heavy wear.

Recommendations: Kent DK from Bare Naked Wools is an absolute favorite of mine, with a 2-ply structure and gentle addition of ultrasoft Merino top. Fancy Tiger's Heirloom Romney (featured in the Heirloom Chevron Baby Blanket, see page 49) comes in a variety of richly dyed colors that show off Romney's heathery versatility, while Stone Wool's softer, sophisticated palette of Romney Merino offers even more options for winter-weight garments.

WENSLEYDALE

I first discovered Wensleydale as a spinning fiber through the Hello Yarn Fiber Club. Adrian Bazilia, dyer and founder of Hello Yarn, has a love for this shimmering fiber, especially when dyed in enticing colors and spun at a gossamer weight for delicate shawls. Wensleydale has a very long staple length, and can be up to 12" (30.5 cm) within a single fleece. This makes it quite tricky for some mills to process, so this fiber is not widely available in yarn form. It is a delightful treat, especially for those who knit lace. The long staple also gives Wensleydale an exceptional amount of sheen that isn't found in shorter fibers.

Recommendations: Blacker Yarns has a wonderful yarn called Tamar Lustre Blend that features Wensleydale alongside several other breeds with similar hand and high shine. Flying Fibers offers a North American Wensleydale spun from its own farm stock that is beautiful used as-is in natural cream.

While you explore these new-to-you wools and fibers, keep an open mind! Trying these wools and diversifying your fiber purchases is a step toward preserving heritage breeds and wool variety for future generations of fiber crafters. Without our support, small fiber farmers will not be able to keep raising these interesting and genetically critical animals.

WOOL FESTIVALS

IN 2015, TWO YEARS BEFORE *Slow Knitting* was published, I was invited by my friend Julie to attend my first-ever NY State Sheep and Wool Festival, affectionately called "Rhinebeck" (the name of the town where the show takes place) by most of the knitting world. This induction into the world of wool festivals could not have been more appropriate or thrilling. I would, for the first time, be in the presence of thousands of other wool lovers, ranchers, farmers, and dyers, all in the same place. I would have the opportunity to connect with online friends I had never met in person, see some exceptional knits, and eat at the famous artichoke stand.

Over the past decade, Rhinebeck has become a mecca for knitters hoping to meet their favorite designers, shop unique yarns that can't be found anywhere else, and snap photos with their knitting friends in front of brilliant foliage. Held in mid-October, this festival comes at the very end of the summer festival season, and sometimes feels as if it is kicking off knitting season in the fall. Many knitters begin working months in advance on a new sweater to wear to the event, and the Rhinebeck Sweater has also served as a jumping-off point for many knitwear designers to debut new patterns.

My first Rhinebeck was perfect in every sense of the word, albeit a little cold for me. It snowed on the second day, and I had to pile on every knit in my luggage to make it from barn to barn, but my memories are nothing if not tinged with golden light. I adored having the ability to interact directly with the people behind my yarn. With more than ten thousand people in attendance, the show was bustling and crowded, but I could find solace and quiet moments in the livestock pens, where sheep slept or bleated in stalls labeled with the breed names. For the first time, I was able to put a wooly face to the names of my favorite yarns, and get a sense of size. Merinos are massive in contrast to tiny, horned Shetlands. I came home energized and ready to turn these behind-the-scenes moments into an all-encompassing passion for knowing my yarn's origin.

Attending a large wool festival is a goal for many and a delightful experience, and attending a wool festival of any size is a special treat. Wool festivals are, first and foremost, celebrations of the relationship between fiber producers and the end consumer. In very few industries are we able to interact directly with the producer of our end product, but at a wool festival you can meet the rancher and the sheep, ask questions, and see for yourself that the fleece or hank you're headed home with comes from a happy place.

By attending, you are encouraging members of your community to take up wool production and education. Many would-be farmers' love of animals begins with a 4-H project, and a bottle lamb, or raising wool sheep to their first shearing, is a wonderful, personal way for children to get acquainted with the needs and challenges of livestock. When we visit a wool festival decked out in finished knits, we're showing producers that their project reaches far beyond the animal they have come to love, and that there is a very tangible appreciation for their product. With heritage breeds slowly disappearing, projects like Shave 'Em to Save 'Em, which encourage the raising of unusual wools and the spinning and knitting of the resulting fiber, potentially get their start with young farmers who feel properly rewarded for their love and attention to raising animals.

Traveling to a wool show is a great way to reconnect with knitting friends. Plan to attend together, and you can rent a home away from home, in a climate different from your own, and spend the evenings knitting and the days exploring booths and stalls. Even if it's too hot to wear knits to the festival, you'll have fun sharing your dreams, and desires for the skeins you bring back, with those who will understand you best. After my first Rhinebeck, I attended several events with friends, and found that my favorite way to travel as a knitter is in a group.

I know of many knitters who have turned to wool festivals as their only occasion to purchase yarn for the whole year. I strive to someday be one of these people, who take only what is offered at their local wool show and turn it into garments they love and can trace from beginning to end. I imagine that working with fibers grown in your climate and area is as beneficial as eating locally grown food or consuming locally gathered honey. It is certainly a wonderful way to get to know the community of makers around you.

wool festival survival guide

It's festival season! Before you whip out your glitter body paint, let me be clear: Late spring to early autumn is *wool* festival season, the magical time of the year when crafters of all stripes travel to sheep-centric events near and far. For the first-time attendee, these events can be overwhelming, so I've put together a little list of handy tips for anyone making their first fiber foray.

WHAT TO WEAR

These festivals often take place on large, unfinished fairgrounds. Some may have hay- or gravel-floored barns, but there's generally a good possibility your shoes will get dirty. You'll also be on your feet all day, so factor that into your choice of footwear. If the festival is taking place after a particularly rainy week, I recommend having a brown paper bag in the trunk and a change of shoes for driving home, too.

While a portion of the festival should be covered, it's possible that you could find yourself walking in drizzling rain or snow, or going in and out of chilly weather from building to building. Bring along an all-weather jacket or poncho (depending on the climate and forecast) so you don't find yourself cold and damp.

FOOD AND DRINK

While many of these events have an abundant vendor lineup, the fair food on offer is often a little less than thrilling, so I recommend packing your own lunch and snacks. For me, there's something wonderful about multitasking while waiting in line or being able to nibble throughout the day, so I go for basic, light foods that won't make me tired. Apples, pears, cheese sticks, mixed nuts, a refillable bottle of water or thermos of coffee are all my standby choices. If you think you might be petting animals, be sure to pack some wet wipes or hand sanitizer, too.

STORAGE ON THE GO

An ample tote bag for storage is a must. It can hold extra layers for dramatic weather changes, keep your snacks, and provide the perfect home for your wallet and purchases. Consider packing a few produce totes for your food that can double as fiber bags when empty, and you'll be able to avoid a buildup of plastic or paper packaging from the vendors. A tote of moderate size with thick straps is best, so that if things get heavy it's not cutting into your shoulders.

PLAN FOR PURCHASES

I'm not the only knitter who has fallen prey to "festival frenzy": spending more than my budget on wool and yarn, snatching up buttons like a madwoman, and eyeing a full fleece that most certainly *will not fit* in my carry-on. Combat these impulses by planning out your purchase budget beforehand and putting that amount, in cash, away in an envelope. Keeping your cash separate from your wallet will also keep you from digging in the tote bag to find it for every purchase. You can pin the envelope just inside the tote bag with a safety pin so it will always be within reach (and under your watchful eye).

It's possible to take it one step further and plan out your pattern choices and projects before you go, too. While it might be tempting to simply save these to Ravelry and access them on your smartphone in the booth, keep in mind that most fairgrounds don't have a strong cellular signal. I recommend pulling up each pattern and project and saving a screenshot to your photos the night before, or writing down your yarn requirements and notes about the pattern (cables, lace, drape, etc.) like a shopping list. If you choose to go the high-technology route, make sure that your phone is fully charged, as it's unlikely you'll find a good spot to charge it within the fairgrounds.

WHERE TO START

Now that you know what to expect, make a list of some upcoming fiber festivals near you. Here are a few of my favorites that take place throughout the year (and a few I have yet to visit, but hope to, soon!).

MARYLAND SHEEP & WOOL FESTIVAL (MDSW)

This festival is one of the largest, and is held in early May in West Friendship, Maryland. Rent spaces in charming nearby Frederick (or bustling Columbia, if you don't mind driving a little bit). At this time of year, rain or chilly weather is likely, so pack a poncho just in case.

NY STATE SHEEP AND WOOL FESTIVAL (RHINEBECK)

Perhaps the most famous of the wool festivals in the United States, this show is known simply as "Rhinebeck" and brings in crowds of more than ten thousand people every year. The mid-October timing makes it perfect for leaf peepers, and rental spaces in Rhinebeck and nearby communities fill up as early as February each year. Plan ahead for this one! I have attended multiple times and have experienced remarkably varied weather, from warm days with temperatures around 65°F (18°C) to bitter cold with snow.

SOUTHEASTERN ANIMAL FIBER FAIR (SAFF)

Held in Fletcher, North Carolina, this festival is probably the top wool event in the southern United States. For many, this October event takes the place of Rhinebeck and offers a more accessible location and an easier pace, while still having tons of vendors, animals, and exciting

yarns on offer. I would recommend staying in nearby Asheville and experiencing the great culture (and food) of the area, although you could certainly drive from Atlanta or Nashville, if desired, for the day.

MAINE FIBER FROLIC

This is one of those wonderful local fiber fairs that has turned into so much more! Given the proximity of Windsor, Maine, to Portland, one of knitting's epicenters, you're likely to see many familiar faces from your favorite knitting books and magazines at this June event.

IOWA SHEEP & WOOL

I couldn't possibly write about wool festivals without plugging this fantastic sheep and wool show in central Iowa. Iowa doesn't get a lot of attention, but once a year, in June, Ames is descended upon by fluffy creatures and fiber lovers. If you're a Midwesterner, visiting this show is a must! Ames is a cute little college town (I used to live there) and has some wonderful local restaurants and plenty of places to stay.

Here are some other potentially great shows that I've heard about (but haven't attended). Ask your favorite fiber people for more recommendations and try to get to at least one—it's always worth it to have a little wool vacation!

Boorowa Irish Woolfest
British Wool Show
Manitoba Fibre Festival
Taos Wool Festival
Vermont Sheep & Wool Festival

GOLDEN HOUR

SUMMER IS FADING, ALTHOUGH IN Tennessee it hangs on so very long, lingering in the air with the humidity like a cloud of gnats by a pond, swirling and miserable. Midway into October, we'll still be struggling along with temperatures around 95°F (35°C), while the rest of the world has already moved on from summer and into autumn, with her enchanting pumpkins and spice candles, flannel, and the promise of sweater weather.

I begin anticipating autumn in September, dreaming of boots and crunchy leaves, the smell of woodsmoke in the air and the start of knitting season, but lately I wonder if I'm rushing things. Although Tennessee's winters are short, I always celebrate the sweetness of summer's arrival. Those first rolling thunderstorms that flash and rumble overhead, dumping buckets of water as warm as a bath—every summer I wind up running through at least one, caught running an errand or on the way home without an umbrella.

When autumn comes, I will miss the damp cool of morning, already promising heat as I work in my tiny patio garden, encouraging plants that I've cultivated from seedlings and praising their efforts to grow larger. With coffee in hand, I sit out on the porch on dewy concrete and watch the world come to life around me. I watch as the cats follow the sun, puddle-jumping from beam to beam as the light moves through the house.

The perfect late summer day is a magical thing, dipped in gold at both ends, a day in August that starts by outlining the world in a glowing nimbus, the light warm, welcoming, and full of promise. Summer days are longer, and the longest ones stretch on and on, allowing us to savor every morning moment spent reading or knitting, every evening moment filled with ice cream and late night conversation.

As the sun sets in mid-October in Tennessee, the light starts to catch in a different way, highlighting little clouds in periwinkle and sky blue, pale pink skeins glowing behind them. The clouds look a bit like winter clouds, heavy and soft like downy blankets. The mornings shift and become a bit cooler and darker, and the sun sets earlier. Golden hour is over, but it was glorious.

autumn equinox

KNITTING SEASON BEGINS

AUTUMN SOMETIMES ARRIVES IN SMALL amounts, taking bites out of summer's golden glory a little at a time. First, the evenings turn cooler, giving us bonfire and camping weather at the end of a muggy season. Then, the mornings retain a bit of that crispness, with lower temperatures lingering even after the sun has risen. The leaves underfoot are suddenly crunchy and abundant, though the trees may not yet have changed color; and all the small animals and birds seem a bit busier, finding new materials to add to their nests in preparation for colder weather. The honking of geese, flying overhead in formation, heralds the change, and a part of my heart stirs. Knitting season is upon us.

In every season, there is room to knit, but autumn accommodates us in new ways. With the temperatures dropping, it is easier on our hands to work with animal fibers that have felt too sticky all summer long: We can once more pick up wool, mohair, alpaca, yak, and Angora with ease and take these projects along with us outside the shelter of air-conditioned spaces. There is an idyllic image in each crafter's head of the perfect knitting moment: Mine features a screened porch in the late afternoon, a throw blanket over my lap, and a cozy cardigan around my shoulders as I make new stitches, one by one, in cool, crisp air tinged with woodsmoke.

The longer mornings and evenings give us a little wiggle room to make. As darkness comes on earlier, I find myself more eager to snuggle up with a project in glowing lamplight after dinner, or under blankets before bed. The mornings also seem better paced. I feel only the call of the kettle and my favorite chair, in which I settle to watch the sun make her slow, soft appearance against foggy landscapes.

The change in the weather means that we can be reunited with our favorite knits. Having carefully put them away in spring, we now unwrap the tissue paper and reveal sweaters, scarves, shawls, and hats; their making is a memory retained in every stitch, and I revisit the time spent with them as I rediscover each one in drawers and storage boxes. I revel in the simple action of putting away the summer things and replacing them with well-loved, cool-weather pieces: stacks of sweaters and rolls of handknit socks in drawers, cascades of wooly scarves in the coat closet.

Having spent the last season gathering inspiration, dyeing yarns, and drawing up plans, I take up my notes in autumn and move them into action. Sketches and swatches become numbers on paper; the printouts or marked pages in pattern books are opened and materials are gathered to begin. My wooden swift and ball winder are ever busy as I eagerly wind hanks into short, squishy cakes that can be stacked, ready for use. After a long work week, it feels especially indulgent to cast on a new sweater on Saturday morning and knit away on it through late Sunday evening. Each wooly stitch—the feel of the fibers slipping through my fingers, the bounce of the yarn as it wraps around the needle—thrills me in new ways. As the fabric grows, I stop frequently and take a better look at it, marveling at the beauty of what I am creating and dreaming of what it will become.

Connecting with our past knits and stash does not need to be a solitary endeavor. This is the perfect moment to meet up with friends who also knit or crochet, an opportunity to revel in the season and build perfect projects together. Digging through and organizing stash, determining the future of a work in progress from a previous season, or gleefully casting on something new are all enhanced in the company of other fiber enthusiasts. I love to invite a fiber friend over for a hearty lunch of stew and crusty bread, followed by a bit of knitting and catching up. Soon, the holidays will be upon us, and it will be harder to make room for friends in the bustle of family obligations—so make the time now.

I always feel that autumn is the shortest season, so above all I seek to celebrate my moment within it, and not rush through. Soon, the breezes that feel refreshing and calming will become more bitter, and my favorite sweaters will need the added protection of a winter coat. For now, I will embrace the fading sunshine, this moment on the precipice of change that coats the world in new color and brings me the desire to reconnect, to rediscover, and to renew the knitter within me.

Loam Hat

/ About the Yarn /

HANDSPUN HOPE: ORGANIC MERINO WOOL YARN

I first met some of the amazing women behind Handspun Hope while visiting a wool show in Chicago. Their booth was simple but bright, and the yarn, nubbly and dense, spoke to me in a way few yarns have, begging to be taken home. Later, I would find out that Handspun Hope is an organization designed to do good for the people of Rwanda, and specifically for the women and children of Rwanda most affected by poverty and genocide. By connecting communities and generations in Rwanda through the process of raising, spinning, and dyeing yarn together, Handspun Hope is contributing to lasting change that will help families prosper.

The organic Merino used for this yarn is from a well-tended flock located near the base of Mount Sabyinyo in northern Rwanda. When the fleeces are shorn, they are sent to the Handspun Hope headquarters, where they are spun into yarns and dyed with a variety of natural dyes native to the area. Eucalyptus, salvia, cosmos, and onion skin are just a few of the materials used to communicate a color story of rich earth tones, golden yellows, and bright oranges—the colors of Rwanda.

SIZES
Small (Medium, Large, X-Large)

FINISHED MEASUREMENTS
18 (20, 22, 24)" [45.5 (51, 56, 61) cm] circumference
Note: *Measurements are taken unstretched; this fabric is dense and sturdy.*

YARN
Handspun Hope Organic Merino Wool Yarn [100% organic Merino wool from Rwanda; 185 yards (169 meters)/4 ounces (100 grams)]: 1 (1, 2, 2) skein(s) Eucalyptus

ALTERNATIVE YARNS
150 (165, 185, 200) yards [137 (151, 169, 183) meters] in a heavy worsted-weight yarn

If you'd like to swap out this yarn, look for yarns that are dense and closely spun, typically a characteristic of small mill production or handspinning techniques. You'll want a heavy, almost aran-weight yarn rather than a worsted weight that leans toward DK weight. Each stitch should feel round and solid. The model is wearing the hat a bit loosely to accommodate full hair, and the sample is the size Large.

(Canada) KINTRA Wool 2-Ply (100% wool; Bluefaced Leicester and Romney blend)

(US) Doc Mason's Wool (100% wool)

(US) Stone Wool Corriedale (100% Corriedale wool)

NEEDLES
Size US 7 (4.5 mm) needle(s) in your preferred style for working in the rnd

Change needle size if necessary to obtain correct gauge.

NOTIONS
Stitch marker

GAUGE
20 sts and 28 rounds = 4" (10 cm) in 1x1 Rib

PATTERN NOTES

Please note that this yarn has a tendency to rub off a bit on whatever needle you use, and light-colored wooden needles may show some color transfer throughout your project.

HAT

Note: Use your preferred method of working in the rnd.

CO 90 (100, 110, 120) sts. Join for working in the rnd, being careful not to twist sts; pm for beginning of rnd.

Rnds 1–18: *K1, p1; repeat from * to end.

Rnd 19: Purl.

Rnd 20: *K2, p3; repeat from * to end.

Rnd 21: *Slip 2, p3; repeat from * to end.

Rnds 22–41: Repeat Rnds 20 and 21 nine more times.

Rnd 42: Knit.

Rnd 43: Purl.

Rnd 44: Knit.

Rnd 45: *Slip 2, p3; repeat from * to end.

Rnd 46: *K2, p3; repeat from * to end.

Rnds 47–56: Repeat Rnds 44 and 45 five more times.

Rnd 57: Knit.

Rnd 58: Purl.

Rnd 59: Knit.

Shape Crown

Rnd 60: *Slip 2, p1, ssp; repeat from * to end—72 (80, 88, 96) sts remain.

Rnd 61: *K2, p2; repeat from * to end.

Rnd 62: *Slip 2, p2; repeat from * to end.

Rnd 63: Purl.

Rnd 64: Knit.

Rnd 65: Repeat Rnd 62.

Rnds 66 and 67: Repeat Rnds 61 and 62 once.

Rnd 68: *K2, p2tog; repeat from * to end—54 (60, 66, 72) sts remain.

Rnd 69: Knit.

Rnd 70: Purl.

Rnd 71: Knit.

Rnd 72: *Slip 2, p1; repeat from * to end.

Rnd 73: *Ssk, p1; repeat from * to end—36 (40, 44, 48) sts remain.

Rnd 74: *Slip 1, p1; repeat from * to end.

Rnd 75: *K1, p1; repeat from * to end.

Rnd 76: *Ssk; repeat from * to end—18 (20, 22, 24) sts remain.

Rnd 77: Knit.

Rnd 78: Repeat Rnd 76—9 (10, 11, 12) sts remain.

Rnd 79: Knit.

Sizes Large and X-Large Only

Rnd 80: *Ssk; repeat from * to last - (-, 1, 0) st(s), k- (-, 1, 0)—6 sts remain.

All Sizes

Cut yarn, leaving an 8" (20.5 cm) tail. Thread tail through remaining sts twice, pull tight, and fasten off.

FINISHING

I found that this yarn had a considerable bit of rub-off while knitting, and so elected to wash the finished hat in a bit of grease-cutting liquid dish soap (rather than wool wash) and warm water, to increase the bloom of the Merino and release any mordants or dyes remaining from the production process.

After washing, lay the finished hat to dry, flipping it over midway to make sure that the damper side gets plenty of circulation. Do not stretch or shape your hat extensively, or it could grow; try to match the brim to your intended finished measurements.

THE MEDITATION
IN UNRAVELING

PULL A SINGLE STITCH LOOSE and the others will follow: a chain reaction to a moment of frustration, disappointment, or dismay. The project we craved and began with hope has unraveled before us like the yarn we're tugging on: It's too big or too small, too short or too long. Or perhaps we've discovered that the color or fiber is just not right to show off the details, and we must start again from scratch. As our project dissolves into a pile of ramen noodle strands, this yarn with a memory and a past should also bring us hope for a new future.

It can be difficult to gaze upon hours and hours of work and pull it apart, but this is a necessary step in our pursuit of slow knitting. When we take the time to choose beautiful materials for our projects, to research and carefully select them, it seems unthinkable to let something as silly as unraveling keep us from realizing their potential. Yet the emotional labor that we as knitters have put into each stitch keeps us from taking the necessary step of starting over. I myself have set aside for months, or even years, projects that didn't turn out exactly as desired, afraid to begin again.

This hesitation has nothing to do with the materials. Most yarns are infinitely more durable than we give them credit for and can handle a good ripping out, as needed. Even those that get a little fuzzy or sad and show slight variation in our in-progress fabrics will often settle when they've had a good finishing bath to relax and remember how they were spun. For this reason, knitting allows us room to start over and try again almost endlessly—we only have to begin.

Getting in the right mood for unraveling is a process similar to preparing for a yoga flow (after all, we are stretching ourselves mentally and emotionally!). Breathe deep before beginning, and steel yourself for the work ahead. I find that a warm beverage, or a glass of wine, helps loosen me up, and pairing unraveling with something visually enjoyable, like a richly costumed period drama, helps make the process move a bit faster.

When unraveling something large, like a sweater, begin where you left off. If you've got an active ball attached, this will be easy, but the task becomes a bit more difficult if you've decided to unravel after seaming, finishing, or wearing the final piece. In the case of pieced garments, refer to your pattern for guidance, working backward through the steps, if you can, to follow your own construction order. Scissors may be required: Have no fear! If you come out with a little less yardage, that's okay. At least at the end you'll have a usable yarn that can become something else you will surely love.

Wind as you go, releasing your stress and strain, and revel in the simple meditation of pulling out each stitch, tugging against the fabric, and winding another yard around the developing ball. Don't allow a bit of a snag or a surprise catch in a seam to derail your process; instead, appreciate this call to attention and embrace it, focusing on the work at hand.

As each ball is finished, I like to hank it up using a niddy noddy or a swift, and set it aside for a bath. When the pile is complete and the project is no more, these skeins go into a sink or tub of warm water that has been swished with my favorite wool wash (or a drop of lavender oil) and soak until the kinks relax. Think of this step as your chance to forgive the wool, and for the wool to forgive you, for time spent on something that never came to fruition. As these skeins dry, they are infused with the warmth of the sun and the freshness of the breeze. Pull down these renewed, plump yarns and dream with them again.

tackling the WIPs

When autumn knitting season comes, I like to pull out my stash of works in progress (WIPs) and see what will be continued into the fall, and what will be repurposed, unraveled, and set aside to be reassigned and become something new. Even if you've already performed this exercise in the spring, I find that by September's arrival there will be a few languishing projects that need to be addressed. I have a system for sorting out my in-progress projects, and I hope you might also find it useful.

EVALUATE THE STATE OF COMPLETION

A sweater we've finished that simply needs to be seamed together, or perhaps have the buttons added on, has been sitting in the "almost finished" basket or shoved into the bag in the back corner of the closet. The steps are simple enough, but we just can't seem to do them: The siren song of casting on something new has been too alluring. Dig these projects out now, as we turn to the new knitting season of the year, and spend an afternoon finishing them up and preparing them for wear. It's the perfect time to show off a recently completed garment.

If you find that this bin is full of ill-fitting things, or colors you'll no longer wear, consider whether you've had your moment with the yarn and need to move on. Sometimes, the time spent unraveling is far longer than the time a bound-off edge requires, and you can put a finished object in your holiday presents pile if it no longer suits.

UNRAVEL THE HOPELESS

I can't count how many projects I began because I felt they'd be the perfect thing for me. In that moment, the moment of casting on, perhaps they did fulfill an important need, but now, looking at the sad, rumpled pile of fabric that would be an ill-fitting sweater, I see that it's time to unravel. Pulling apart a nearly completed project is a big undertaking, but there are ways to make it a little easier.

If you already know how you'd repurpose the yarn, go ahead and unravel the entire garment, carefully taking apart seamed pieces and hand-winding the yarn back into a ball. You can hank, soak, and dry it later, and it will be as good as new. (For more on this process, see page 106.)

If the yarn is no longer to your liking, offer the semicompleted project to a knitting friend or on an online trading site for free or a low, reasonable price. It's unlikely the buyer will knit the same project you have, but they might be willing to unravel for the purpose of free yarn or yarn they would like to try but that is usually too expensive. Make sure you include any relevant information and any labels you're able to hunt down, and double-check to make sure there's no evidence of pest damage. The most embarrassing thing in the world would be to infest someone else's stash with a problem you didn't know you had!

DIG INTO OLD PASSIONS

While exploring these works in progress, be open to the idea that one of them could entice you to begin it anew. Make sure you check for notes on the project if you've got a paper pattern in the same project bag; there may have been some alterations you made that you've forgotten about. In addition, count the stitches before beginning and make sure there wasn't a mistake that caused you to stop and that needs to be addressed before you move forward.

If you find yourself romanced by a past project, embrace it, and love the one you're with for a while. Working without the burden of a full project basket can be a beautiful thing.

reviving used yarns

If you're among the knitters who believe that this once-knit yarn is now a kinky, tangled mess beyond salvaging, know that you are not alone! I cannot count how many knitters I've talked to who believe that the little bit of yarn in their swatch, or the yarn unwound from a previous project, must be thrown away or used as waste yarn. I have wonderful news: This yarn is absolutely not damaged, and there is a process to restore it to its original condition, making it suitable for creating new things, in your hands or the hands of someone else.

UNTANGLE IT

If the skein you have is tangled, take the time to gently work your way through winding it back into a ball by hand. A hand-wound ball is the best method for detangling, as the ball is easily maneuvered through loops, and a swift or ball winder is not. Once you have the hand-wound ball, you'll have done the hardest part of restoring the yarn.

MAKE A HANK

As a spinner, I have a delightful tool, called a niddy noddy, that makes this step in the process easier. If you also have one, you already know how to make a hank—but if you don't own a niddy noddy, you can create a hank on the widest part of the back of a wooden chair. Begin winding the yarn around the back of the chair, keeping each wrap close together and snug so it doesn't slip down or move. After winding all the yarn onto the chair, tie each end around all the strands, bundling them on each side of the loop you've created. Pull the loop upward and off the chair. Add an extra tie or two with undyed or light-colored waste yarn to secure the loop.

SOAK

Fill a sink or washtub with warm water and a little wool soap (this will also have the added benefit of cleaning off any oils from your hands, or any body lotions, that may have been transferred to your knitting while you were working with it the first time). Allow the hank to fully submerge in the water and soak for thirty minutes to an hour. Drain the water and gently push out as much remaining water as possible, then transfer to a drying rack outdoors or position in the bathtub to allow the hank to dry.

POP

Once the hank is dry, lift it from the drying rack and place a hand into each side of the loop and hold the hank taut (enough so that you could clap your hands in the middle, but the hank would slide down your arms if you tried). Begin "popping" the skein by letting the tension on the loop relax slightly, then bringing it back suddenly with your hands. This will fluff the fibers a little bit so they look fresh and clean.

TWIST

Keeping your hands inside the loop, begin to make a circle, with your right and left hands moving in the same direction, adding twist to the loop so that it begins to coil up on itself. When it reaches a comfortable but tight level of tension, pull one end of the hank slightly through the other end, and the loop should coil back perfectly into a twisted skein.

LABEL

If you're the type to save labels, consider reattaching them with a bit of string to each skein or the skein bundle so you'll remember what the yarn is when you want to work with it later. If you know you'll be casting on soon, you could also preassign a project bag and needle and have the yarn and your pattern all in the same place.

MAKE DO AND MEND

WE LIVE IN A CULTURE that used to spend a lot more time repairing and fixing things. In Appalachia, the region I and my ancestors have long called home, tinkering with broken objects is a point of pride as well as a pastime. Eyesores though they are, lawns piled up with ailing lawnmowers, tractors, and cars are not uncommon in rural Tennessee, North Carolina, and Virginia. Look closely and you'll notice that these machines are often the same make and model, carefully arranged and collected as stores of old parts.

This type of collecting is not exclusive to those who live in the hollers of my home state; I notice it when I travel north and visit American mills still in operation, too. The machines that run in these mills are aging, as are the hands that still know how to operate and repair them. Almost every mill I've visited has a hodgepodge parts room: cogs, gears, wheels, and other clunky bric-a-brac, cannibalized from long-gone machines and crucial to keeping the machinery running. Often, new parts simply aren't attainable, and would need to be custom-made—an expensive process that would also require the machine to be shut down. Lost time means lost money, so the mills collect old equipment as it comes on the market, but the acquisition is bittersweet. A new piece for one machine means that another machine, somewhere, has ceased running.

Clothing, ever since the Industrial Revolution allowed us to begin producing it cheaper and faster, has not retained this sense of usefulness and value. While it was once a common practice to cut up old clothes to make quilts, it's not unusual now to see quilters carefully collecting stacks of fat quarters, perfectly color-coordinated and ready to be made into crisp, fresh bedding. The fabrics our clothes are made of now have been designed to last longer than their original counterparts—polyester and rayon are slow-fading, and don't degrade quickly—and yet we have them sewn into garments that will fall apart at the seams within a few seasons, and the fabric is rarely repurposed.

We are lucky to be knitters in this time. There is certainly a developed market for knitting yarns that feature plastic-based synthetics and their modern wonders of performance: They are pilling- and stain-resistant, and their vibrant color never fades. Somehow, though, knitters have also managed to preserve natural fibers and our access to them. Perhaps the call of wool is a little too strong to be drowned out by capitalism, or perhaps the simple, earnest versatility of animal fibers is the explanation. We see the value in these fibers when we are working with them: their softness in our hands, their connection to the earth and the creatures that were involved in their production. The finished fabric, delightfully bouncy and light, yet warm. A knitter who works frequently with wonderful natural fibers will never dream of seeking a synthetic replacement.

Why is it that the value we attribute to these natural fibers doesn't always extend to caring for and preserving what they become?

I am astonished, always, when knitters in my classes and workshops assert that they no longer choose a particular yarn because it pills, or that they never knit socks because they will wear holes into the heels. These are not insurmountable challenges: They are the simple reality of well-loved objects. We have to expect more of ourselves and our knitting than to make things that will last forever, and we must learn to repair them.

I once had a knitter in a sock workshop who claimed to be an avid sock knitter, but she had never darned a pair. Each time a sock wore thin in the heel or toe, she would simply toss the pair and knit a new set from her extensive stash. It breaks my heart to think of the amount of time she threw away with each sock: not only the time she spent knitting but the time it took to dye the yarn, to carefully shear the fiber, to raise the sheep and see the first fleece grow. The relics of our knitting practice should not be relegated to the trash when they require a little extra work on our part.

Mending isn't difficult, and darning extends far beyond socks: It can be used to heal a worn-out elbow in a beloved cardigan, or secure the underarm of a sleeve that has gotten thin due to heavy wear. With the trend toward visible mending that seems to be sweeping through craft circles, darning offers a new way to experiment and play with fiber; a woven darn becomes a tiny tapestry, a bit of portable art. A knitted patch in a contrasting color begs for a bit of embroidery. By embracing the need to fix, to tinker, and to mend, we push the boundaries of what is acceptable in fashion, and also of what is acceptable to us.

Darning

I've actually come to really appreciate and enjoy the amount of time spent darning knits. With the rising trend toward visible mending and the constant outpouring of creativity from the internet knitting culture, I'm never short on interesting new ways to darn—contrasting colors, faux-plaid weavings, and intarsia-adorned patches are a few ways to dress up this process of mending. In the end, though, darning is an adornment created out of the necessity to close a hole or weak spot in a well-loved knit, and anything that keeps our handmade garments in rotation longer should be welcomed, not resisted.

There are two main types of darns: woven darns and patch darns. You can use these interchangeably to close a hole or secure a developing weak spot in the fabric of your knits. Both are simple to do and require only a few materials: a darning needle (I prefer the type with a curved tip, which is just easier to get in and out of the fabric) and some sort of brace that goes inside the fabric to hold it taut. Darning eggs and mushrooms are some commonly used, wood-turned objects that fulfill the need of a brace, but a tennis ball or golf ball can do just as well in a pinch.

PATCH DARN

The patch darn is a wonderful way to seal up a larger hole, or to cover a weak spot that is sure to wear through. Here, I've applied it to the heel of a beloved pair of handspun socks. As the stitches wear through on the inside, they'll felt up against the edges of the darn and reinforce the patch. If you've got sensitive heels, you can also work a patch on the inside of the sock, for double-durability and a smoother edge against your skin.

First, you'll insert your darning egg into the sock and move it to the area that you want to darn. The egg will act as a brace to highlight the thin stitches so you'll know where to put the darn, and also does the job of stretching out the fabric similarly to how it stretches on your heel (making for a darn that fits well and doesn't pull in any odd directions on the foot while wearing).

Since this is a knitted darn, you'll need two double pointed needles in a similar size to your sock's knitting gauge. You don't need to be exact, just close. You'll begin the process of patch darning by picking up the stitches at the upper edge of the weak spot in your fabric—the first row where the stitches are solid and don't appear to be damaged. You will be knitting from this needle, so try to take the stitches from the same side of each knitted column each time (the right or left side of each stitch).

Take a length of yarn that is the same weight as your original fabric—I've begun to collect leftovers from each project on an embroidery

bobbin card and I store them together for this purpose, but you can use yarn you have in your stash for contrast if you like. Here, I'm showing this fingering weight yarn double-stranded, as I didn't have an exact match for the handspun yarn this project was originally made in.

Begin knitting across the first row of stitches you've just picked up, using your yarn single- or double-stranded as preferred to match the weight of the gauge in your original project. When you come to the end of the first row, you'll turn the work to continue working flat (purling) across the back of the patch.

At this point, pick up a stitch from the next column (up the side) of the next row of your darning area. This moves the patch up for the next row as you create more fabric.

Purl this stitch together with the first stitch of your row so that the patch stays an even size, then purl across all of the patch stitches to the last stitch in the row.

Slip the last stitch onto the right needle, then pick up a stitch from the next column, one row up, from the row you've just worked. Slip the unworked patch stitch back to the left hand needle, and purl (this is like an ssp).

FINISHING

Weave in the remaining ends securely.

WOVEN DARN

Woven darns offer endless possibilities for color play and texture, since they are essentially a plain weave over a bit of your knitting. Use them to secure weak areas or reweave the fabric to cover a hole. Play with plaids or contrasting colors, or use the original yarn for a darn that hides your work and wears similarly to the original material's fabric.

The only materials you'll need to perform this darn are your fabric to be darned, some kind of brace in the form of a darning egg, mushroom, or ball, yarn, and a tapestry needle.

Begin by placing your darning mushroom, egg, or other brace into the fabric you'll be darning. I've used a darning mushroom here because the hole in my fabric is rather large, and I'll want the increased surface area that this shape provides.

You're going to create a miniature plain weave (1 over, 1 under) by creating your own warp and weft threads across the darn. Start by running some of the yarn across the fabric with a tapestry needle in a single direction, spaced one stitch apart, and securing the stitches into the undamaged edges of the darning area. After you've created the warp, you can come back from the alternate direction and weave over 1, under 1, across the lines to create a fabric.

FINISHING

Weave in the remaining ends securely.

WAKE UP
YOUR KNITWEAR

THE TIME HAS COME TO dig out our favorite woolens and put them back in circulation for daily wear! If you've prepared your knits for storage as outlined in the spring cleaning section of this book (see page 15), it will be easy to integrate your favorite pieces; if not, there are a few tricks you can use to wake up your knitwear and make sure every garment is ready to shine all season long.

Even knits that have been stored in tissue with sachets might be a bit musty, so it's best to open them up a week or two before you're ready to wear them—as summer draws to a close, keep an eye on your weather forecast for the right time. Unwrap items and air them out on hangers or on a drying rack for a couple of days to let any lingering scents dissipate. During this time, you can also inspect for any signs of insect or pest presence, reviewing items that have been stored together for holes or damage. If you find small holes or black specks, these could be anything from mouse poop (gross, but washable) to insect casings. If you suspect the latter, put the items in bags and into the freezer for a week, then pull them out and carefully handwash, dry, and return them back to the freezer for another week. This should kill anything that might still be living on the garment, and salvage it.

If you find holes from snags, or weak spots in the fabric, this is the perfect time to mend them. Search your stash scraps for any yarns that match, or, if you've been good and saved a bit of your project yarn, you can pull it out for this purpose. Choose to darn with patches for spots where the fibers have worn completely through, and use the woven darning method for thin areas that haven't quite fallen apart. (For instructions for each, see page 110.) I don't like to throw any knits out, but if they're on the third or fourth darn and involve more repair than the original project did knitting, and the repairs are wearing thin, it might be time to repurpose the fabric for sachets.

Use this time to de-pill your knits, too. My preferred de-pilling tool is a nylon, stiff-bristled brush. You can buy brushes designed specifically for this purpose, or a cheap, free toothbrush from the dentist will do a decent job (though it's a bit slower). I avoid electric sweater shavers at all costs: These actually cut through the pills standing out from the fabric and can weaken the areas that have been shaved, making them more likely to pill later and wear through into holes. I also avoid any tool that pulls too hard or is rough on the fabric.

Remove pills effectively by stretching the area taut and brushing, in short strokes, in a single direction. It might take a while, but if you combine this chore with television time or an audio book, the work goes by a little faster. It's always sad to me when knitters don't devote the same time to maintain their beautiful, finished garments that they do to make them, and a little attention can restore your knits to the same condition they were in when fresh off the needles.

If you didn't follow the storage steps in the spring cleaning section, you may need to give your pieces a seasonal bath. This is best done when the weather is still a little warm, so that you can hang wet pieces to dry outside in the sunshine on garment drying racks. Soaking your socks, sweaters, and accessories in a warm bath in the tub or a large sink is all it takes to have them smelling fresh and ready for wear. Add a few droplets of your favorite essential oil to the water, plus some no-rinse wool wash, for knits that smell fresh longer. I wash my sweaters and accessories only once a year, with the exception of hats, handwarmers, and socks; these items have a tendency to get a little dirtier and so I recommend washing them more frequently. If you live in a particularly cold climate, wash your hats and any cowls that touch your face once or twice a month, since you're breathing (and sometimes sweating) on them a little more. Handwarmers should be washed whenever they start looking a little dirty, and I typically wash my handknit socks every other week (depending on the moisture level of your feet, you may want to wash at shorter intervals).

Handwashing is not that difficult, and it's easy to keep it from feeling like a chore if you mix it into your other weekend activities. Fill a basin or sink with warm water and set the pieces in there for thirty minutes to an hour, then come back later, drain the tub, and squish the water out. Anything that needs heavy blocking requires a little bit of advance planning, but most knits are pretty simple: Just hang or lay flat to dry and they'll be good to go!

Freshen up your sachets from storage by massaging them with your hands and adding a few drops of essential oil of lavender, patchouli, or rosemary to the outer fabric, then toss them into your sweater drawers—they'll be there to keep your sweaters fresh and keep any critters at bay, and will be right where you need them next spring when it's time to store them again.

Occasionally, opening up last season's garments might reveal to you that some of your knits just aren't getting the love they deserve. It happens to all of us: We make something highly anticipated, enjoy the process, then discover that the finished piece just doesn't fit within our wardrobe. If this is the case with any of your knits, use this opportunity to freshen them up and prepare them for either gifting at the holidays or donating. This is the perfect time of year to donate hats, scarves, mittens, handwarmers, and socks to shelters. Soon, the weather will turn and many people will be in need of cold-weather gear. Some shelters will accept donations only of washable yarns—if this is the case, and all your pieces are made from wool or other natural fibers, consider handing them out yourself. There are even movements in some cities of knitters who hang knitted accessories on statues and fences in high-traffic areas with tags inviting those who need the knits to take them home.

This time of year is about the excitement of casting on, but also about reconnecting with some of our favorite pieces, and taking pride in wearing them. These little steps will ensure that your knits look their best (and that you do, too)!

blocking garments

As someone who has lived most of my adult life in fairly small apartments, I have found the finishing of a large object, like a sweater, significantly more daunting than the knitting of it. A sweater knit in pieces can be folded, rolled, and even stuffed into a project bag; even a whole sweater, worked as a single piece in the round with sleeves added near the end, is easy to store. The idea of blocking something large—finishing it up at the end of the process, or preparing pieces to be seamed—seems impossible if you don't have just the right tools or the perfect space for laying things out. Over time, I've developed a few techniques that have made this process for me a little easier, and I think they're probably equally useful for knitters with a bit more space as they are for those of us living in smaller ones.

For garments that are knit in pieces and then seamed, don't feel pressure to pin out and block every piece in a single go. The patterns for these type of garments often have schematics—use them as a guide and pin out single pieces one at a time to match the measurements on the schematic, then double-check before seaming. If you're worried about pieces shifting while you store them (I store mine carefully folded on a shelf), you can always block pieces that go together next to each other before they are seamed: a back and a front together, then sleeves, so that you can seam them up as you go. This can also help the entire seaming process seem a little less overwhelming.

For flat pieces that are not double-layered, you can use children's foam play mats or garage mats (the kind that interlock) and anti-rust T-pins to pin out each piece and measure as you go. If you lack either, you can also pin out and block on a towel. Use the towel as a blocking fabric, sliding your pins into both knitted piece and towel instead of poking them in vertically, and you can hang the towel over the back of a door or shower curtain rod to dry overnight. If you want to block all your pieces at once, this is a great solution for small spaces or the lack of a flat, large area to lay everything out. Of course, the ideal scenario is that you have a blocking mat or foam mat, you pin out all the pieces, and then you are able to put a small fan on them overnight to help everything dry.

A tool that I have found especially helpful for finishing off sweaters that don't require aggressive blocking—like simple pullovers or cardigans—is a handheld steamer. You can find these at any major retailer that has a laundry section, and usually for a very reasonable price. (Don't bother with the standing kind with the large water reservoir unless you're regularly steaming dozens of garments at a time.) A good steaming will resolve uneven tension over Stockinette areas, smooth out any wrinkles or folds, and help the halos on mohair, alpaca, and Angora rise to the surface of the fabric.

Take the time to prepare or purchase some padded hangers for this purpose. When steaming heavily on a standard, hard hanger, you can accidentally stretch out the shoulders (especially on garments that lack shoulder seams for added stability). A padded hanger stands in for your shoulder, keeping the sweater's shoulders in place and rounding out the apex of the sleeve so that it doesn't form odd points.

Lastly, when you know you'll be picking up or adding on stitches, as for a button band or collar, block the entire piece before doing so. It will result in a cleaner pick-up edge and less warbling or waving in the added-on piece, and you can block the new element to match the original a little easier than you can block a whole garment to match a single addition.

Go forth, and fearlessly block your garments! A tiny space is no longer an excuse not to knit exactly what you want to wear.

building a slow wardrobe

I strongly believe that there is a particular hue of every color for every person and taste, and the work that I've done with yarn has helped reinforce this belief. I have spent most of my decade-long yarn career working on developing great shipments of yarn subscriptions—helping push knitters and crocheters of all levels out of their comfort zones to try new techniques, fibers, and colors. I've also learned a lot about the colors we'll wear and the ones most people are uncomfortable with, and how to find your ideal hue within each color family.

For an example, I'll use orange. Bright, true orange (like the color of the fruit) is often cited as the least favorite color, and the most unwearable: It reminds us of traffic cones and safety equipment and candy corn. If you shift orange a bit for a variety of different undertones, however, it's easy to discover oranges that you'll be happy to knit and wear.

Add red to a true orange and you get a sexy, laquer-red vermilion that will create something show-stopping and classic. Darken it some and mute it to discover deep rusty tones that look good on almost anyone but are especially nuanced on folks with warm skin tones. Take it all the way up for a playful sorbet, beige it out for a warm neutral, or add some pink for a soft peach. All these colors are orange; and once you identify your orange, you can formulate a plan to add it to your wardrobe.

While slow knitting is about cutting back on our rush to make and our rush to collect, and about spending time with the projects we've already planned, I've found it nearly impossible to stop buying yarn altogether. I have set certain goals for myself—to buy only what I will use, to have a project planned for every acquisition, and to only fill gaps in my stash—but, through color, I've discovered a loophole. You see, I have a deep, passionate love of color—often, it's the color of a particular yarn that hooks me, and color that makes me crave it, think about it later, and dream about garments that might be perfect in it.

Therefore, it makes sense that color is the principle I now use to collect yarn for future projects. I won't allow myself to buy multiples of the same color for garments—after all, how many dark green sweaters does one need?—so I fill gaps in my sweater stash rainbow when I buy yarn, restricting myself to buying only tones that I don't already have. This sounds fairly limitless, but since we are all a bit restricted in what colors we can wear, it has actually resulted in a beautiful, streamlined palette to work from—and the promise of a wardrobe full of sweaters I can't wait to make and wear.

I've also restricted myself to buying only yarns for garments I will get a lot of wear out of. I don't relish knitting tanks, tops, and tees, but in Tennessee's long summer season I am most likely to get significant use out of these lightweight garments. In addition, delicate cardigans that help me duck in and out of air-conditioned spaces are a must-have for my climate. I find myself considering this as I purchase yarn, reserving my heavier sweater selections for deep-winter, cozy pieces, and selecting more fingering-weight blends that have an added bit of silk, hemp, or linen for transitional weather.

Shape should also be an end consideration. It's easy to fall into the appeal of a popular trend, but not everyone looks good in fitted garments, or in oversize ones. You've had enough time to know what you feel good in; look at some of your favorite store-bought or thrifted pieces and see what shapes you love to wear, then choose your sweater projects accordingly. I have found that navigating away from trends and only toward garments that feel like my personal style ensures longer-lasting success and appreciation

of my knits season after season. Jumping from trend to trend each shopping cycle is a fast-fashion habit that is worth breaking.

Before you select what projects you'll add to your roster, it can also be helpful to look at what you already have and wear the most. Do you prefer a pullover when the weather gets cold, or are cardigans more versatile? When you reach for your favorites, are they casual or dressy? What kind of neckline do you prefer or feel most comfortable in? Where do you like the hem of your sweater to land? These are all helpful questions that will lead you down the path to success when knitting garments!

Above all, remember that you're here to spend time making, not just time wearing, and don't rush through any project. The details count: Weave in your ends with care, choose the perfect buttons, and add little custom touches that make your piece feel finished. I have become quite fond of a small ribbon label, stitched with my initials, or a fold-over leather wrap that can be attached to any hem. Find something special to set your garments apart, or let their simple, subtle presence be enough. The beauty of it all is that everything you make can be exactly what you've desired.

EARLY AUTUMN WALKS

THERE IS A ROMANCE TO early autumn, and perhaps we feel this atmospheric alteration all the more keenly because it has been long anticipated: It is autumn weather we dream about in the heat of summer and the depths of winter.

The brightness of birds once again becomes apparent, as they cluster around a newly filled feeder to peck at sunflower seeds, now eager for distraction since the minding of eggs and fledglings has passed. So, too, we dream of reconnecting with our knitting circle, many of whom will have scattered and traveled for much of the summer season, but return home with new stories to share in the warm glow of friendship.

We may be reunited, at last, with our favorite knits, pulled out of storage and ready for use once more. Greet the crisp breezes of fall with an elegantly wrapped scarf; the chill on your fingers with some well-appointed handwarmers. The crunch of leaves underfoot can only be improved by the addition of knitted socks inside your boots, and pulling on a beloved sweater feels a bit like reuniting with a friend who has been away. Autumn is the time for us to showcase the projects we've made throughout the year.

I revel in the slow build of every early fall day. Nippy, chilly mornings are perfect for cozying up. While the scent of freshly brewed coffee permeates the kitchen, I watch the soft glow of sunlight warm each blade of grass and fading flower. Wrapping myself in a blanket and my fingers around a mug, I use these morning moments as perfect opportunities to get a few stitches in before the day begins, a feline friend resting at my feet or on my lap.

In Tennessee, our days warm up gradually, and by midday it could almost be a more comfortable version of our summer. The light is golden and warm, and the world outside seems to resonate with a feeling of appreciation for what will soon fade into winter's chill. This is the perfect time of day to move my work outside, to take a walk. The sunlight glitters through the changing leaves on every tree, and the woods that run beside the creek have the soft, earthen smell of leaf detritus. I listen to the sounds around me intently—the quiet swish of the slow-moving water, the insistent call of each blue jay and cackling crow. I will carry these golden days with me into winter, and dream of early autumn walks.

Friendship Bracelet Cardigan

/ About the Yarn /

HARRISVILLE DESIGNS: SHETLAND

If there is a more idyllic and knitterly location than Harrisville, New Hamsphire, I've yet to visit it. This tiny town, built up around the Harrisville Woolen Mills in 1794, is a cluster of red-brick buildings, centered around the peaceful Harrisville Pond, and still houses many members of the Colony family, who have owned and operated the mill since the mid-1800s. Other buildings in the town have been preserved with the help of the Historic Harrisville nonprofit, and this area seems almost stopped in time, especially when you visit during the golden splendor that is autumn in New England.

For the past two years, I've had the honor of teaching in the studio space above the retail store here, and it is one of my favorite places to return. In addition to the wonderful students and exceptional staff at Harrisville, I've always felt welcomed by the town: The folks working at the general store, the magic of quiet walks along the side of the pond, the crispness of autumn in the air. I have dreamed deeply of taking up residence in New Hampshire, and someday, I will. For now, I've had to settle for bringing back sweater lots of deliciously sheepy, woolen-spun yarn that Harrisville Designs produces.

Shetland is a classic yarn for Harrisville and is similar to many beloved woolen-spun yarns from around the globe with a central purpose: providing crafters with an exceptional color selection in the form of a workhorse, toothy wool. Unlike some of its British and Scandinavian counterparts, I find that Shetland (and the heavier Highland) soften beautifully with only a single wash. Spun on historic carding machines, each colorway is a careful blending of pre-dyed wool, and the resulting yarn has depth and character as a result. Foliage, the color chosen for this sweater's base, is a perfect match to fading, golden leaves of late fall.

SIZES

To fit bust sizes 34-36 (38-40, 42-44, 46-48) (50-52, 54-56, 58-60, 62-64)" [86.5-91.5 (96.5-101.5, 106.5-112, 117-122) (127-132, 137-142, 147.5-152.5, 157.5-162.5) cm]

FINISHED MEASUREMENTS

42½ (47, 51¼, 55¾) (58½, 63, 67¼, 71¾)" [108 (119.5, 130, 141.5) (148.5, 160, 171, 182) cm], buttoned

YARN

Harrisville Designs Shetland [100% virgin wool, sourced in Australia and New Zealand, domestically milled; 217 yards (198 meters)/1.8 ounces (50 grams)]: 7 (8, 8, 9) (9, 10, 10, 11) skeins Foliage (MC); approx 30 yards (27.5 meters) of each accent color (you'll want at least 2 yards (2 meters) per braid]. I used accent colors Oatmeal, White, Adobe, Loden Blue, Russet, and Charcoal.

ALTERNATIVE YARNS

1,515 (1,635, 1,730, 1,805) (1,925, 2,020, 2,130, 2,235) yards [1,385 (1,495, 1,582, 1,650) (1,760, 1,847, 1,948, 2,044) meters] in a fingering weight yarn

(Norway) Rauma Finullgarn
(100% wool)

(UK) Jamieson's Shetland Spindrift (100% Shetland wool)

(US) Elemental Affects Natural
Shetland Fingering (100% North
American Shetland wool)

In the case of Harrisville Designs
Shetland, the term "Shetland"
refers to a classic method of
spinning for colorwork and not to
the content of the yarn. However, there are several Shetland
wool yarns I have recommended
above if you'd like to try a more
traditional combination of weight
and texture. Additionally, any fingering-weight yarn where you are
able to get appropriate gauge is
a great stand-in for this sweater
(yes, even smoothly spun yarns,
although they may have more
drape in the finished piece).
Above all, swatching is key here
and a fun way to play with braid
combinations.

NEEDLES

Size US 6 (4 mm) circular needle
and needle(s) in your preferred
style for working in the rnd

Change needle size if necessary
to obtain correct gauge.

NOTIONS

Stitch markers, including 1 in a
unique color or style for beginning of rnd; removable stitch
markers; stitch holders or waste
yarn; crochet hook size US F-5
(3.75 mm), for finishing the steek;
six ¾" (19 mm) buttons

GAUGE

18 sts and 30 rounds = 4"
(10 cm) in Flat Double Moss
Stitch, after blocking

STITCH PATTERNS

CIRCULAR 2×2 RIB
(multiple of 4 sts; 1-rnd repeat)
All Rnds: *K2, p2; repeat from *
to end.

FLAT 2×2 RIB
(multiple of 4 sts; 2-row repeat)
Row 1 (RS): K3, *p2, k2; repeat
from * to last st, k1.
Row 2: P3, *k2, p2; repeat from *
to last st, p1.
**Repeat Rows 1 and 2 for Flat 2×2
Rib.**

CIRCULAR DOUBLE MOSS
STITCH
Rnd 1: *K2, p2; repeat from * to
end.
Rnd 2: Knit the knit sts and purl
the purl sts as they face you.
Rnd 3: Knit the purl sts and purl
the knit st as they face you.
Rnd 4: Repeat Rnd 2.
**Repeat Rnds 1–4 for Circular
Double Moss Stitch.**

FLAT DOUBLE MOSS STITCH
(multiple of 2 sts + 4; 4-row
repeat)
Row 1 (RS): K2, *p2, k2; repeat
from * to end.
Row 2: Knit the knit sts and purl
the purl sts as they face you.
Row 3: Knit the purl sts and purl
the knit sts as they face you.
Row 4: Repeat Row 2.
**Repeat Rows 1–4 for Flat Double
Moss Stitch.**

RIGHT-LEANING LATVIAN
BRAID
Use 2 colors of your choice, designated here as A and B.
Rnd 1: *K1 with A, k1 with B;
repeat from * to end.
Rnd 2: With both colors held to
front, p1 with A, bring B under A
in your hand, p1 with B; bring A
under B in your hand, p1 with A.
Continue in this manner, always
bringing new color under previous
color, until you have completed
the rnd.
Rnd 3: With both colors held to
front, p1 with A, bring B over A
in your hand, p1 with B; bring A
over B in your hand, p1 with A.
Continue in this manner, always
bringing new color over previous
color, until you have completed
the round.

LEFT-LEANING LATVIAN BRAID

Use 2 colors of your choice, designated here as A and B.

Rnd 1: *K1 with A, k1 with B; repeat from * to end.

Rnd 2: With both colors held to front, p1 with A, bring B over A in your hand, p1 with B; bring A over B in your hand, p1 with A. Continue in this manner, always bringing new color over previous color, until you have completed the rnd.

Rnd 3: With both colors held to front, p1 with A, bring B under A in your hand, p1 with B; bring A under B in your hand, p1 with A. Continue in this manner, always bringing new color under previous color, until you have completed the rnd.

PATTERN NOTES

This sweater has a raglan construction, with a very open, classic armhole and boxy body. It is worked in the round and then steeked into a cardigan, and makes a great first steeking project. I've shortened the length of the body slightly to give it a more modern, jacket-like look and have added a Latvian Braid detail to the neckline, hem, and cuffs. These braids, worked in a variety of coordinating or surprising colors, remind me of the embroidery-floss friendship bracelets exchanged with your dearest friend at the end of a long summer. Choose your colors in a way that makes you happy or uses up scraps. The Latvian braid technique at this gauge presents a braid roughly ¼" (6 mm) in width, so stack as many as you like at the cuffs to give yourself a full or dainty look (I went with 5 on each sleeve).

When setting up the raglan pattern, you may not complete the last repeat of Double Moss Stitch before working the raglan stitch.

SPECIAL TECHNIQUES

Long-Tail CO: Leaving tail with about 1" (2.5 cm) of yarn for each stitch to be cast on, make a slipknot in the yarn and place it on the right-hand needle, with the tail to the front and the working end to the back. Insert the thumb and forefinger of your left hand between the strands of yarn so that the working end is around your forefinger and the tail end is around your thumb, "slingshot" fashion; *insert the tip of the right-hand needle into the front loop on the thumb, hook the strand of yarn coming from the forefinger from back to front, and draw it through the loop on your thumb; remove your thumb from the loop and pull on the working yarn to tighten the new stitch on the right-hand needle; return your thumb and forefinger to their original positions and repeat from * for remaining sts to be cast on.

Finishing the Steek: When the piece is dry, reinforce the stitch columns one stitch in from each edge of the steek (stitch columns 2 and 4 of the steek) as follows: Using MC yarn (you may use a different yarn, but make sure it is a yarn that will felt or it will not hold the stitches securely; stickier yarns, not superwash yarns, make the best steek reinforcement) and a crochet hook, make a slipknot on the hook; beginning with the first st in the first column to be reinforced, *insert the hook into the center of the stitch in the knit column, draw up a loop, yarn over the hook, and draw the loop through the 2 stitches on the hook (1 stitch remains on the hook); repeat from * until all stitches in the column have been reinforced. Repeat for the second column. You will now have one stitch column in the center with a crochet chain reinforcement on each side. Slide a piece of cardboard or a cutting mat into the body of the sweater before cutting the steek (this will prevent you from cutting through any other part of the sweater by accident). With a sharp pair of scissors, cut down the center of the steek, being careful to cut only through the very center of the stitch column.

NECKBAND

With MC, using the Long-Tail CO or preferred stretchy but sturdy CO of your choice, CO 79 (79, 83, 87) (91, 95, 99, 103) sts. Join for working in the rnd, being careful not to twist sts; pm unique marker for beginning of rnd.

Set-Up Rnd: K5, pm for end of steek sts, k2, *p2, k2; repeat from * to end.

Work even until piece measures ½" (1.3 cm) from the beginning.

Next Rnd: K1, using 2 colors of your choice, work Rnd 1 of Left-Leaning Latvian Braid to end. Work even until braid is complete.

Shape Raglan

Note: *When working Double Moss Stitch, you may not complete the last pattern repeat before working the raglan st.*

Set-Up Rnd: K5, sm, work 11 (11, 12, 13) (14, 15, 16, 17) sts in Double Moss Stitch, k1 (left front raglan st), pm, k1 (left sleeve raglan st), work 10 sts in Double Moss Stitch, k1 (left sleeve raglan st), pm, k1 (right back raglan st), work 24 (24, 26, 28) (30, 32, 34, 36) sts in Double Moss Stitch, k1 (left back raglan st), pm, k1 (right sleeve raglan st), work 10 sts in Double Moss Stitch, k1 (right sleeve raglan st), pm, k1 (right front raglan st), work in Double Moss Stitch to end.

Shape Back Neck

Note: *Change to Flat Double Moss Stitch, beginning with row following last rnd worked.*

Short-Row 1 (RS): K5, sm, work as established across left front, left sleeve, then back sts, to 1 st before fourth marker (between back and right sleeve), turn.

Short-Row 2 (WS): Slip 2 sts purlwise wyif, work to 1 st before third marker (between back and left sleeve), turn.

Short-Row 3: Slip 2 sts purlwise wyib, work to 2 sts before last gap, turn.

Short-Row 4: Slip 2 sts purlwise wyif, work to 2 sts before last gap, turn.

Repeat Short-Rows 3 and 4 twice more.

Resolution Rnd 1: Work in patterns as established to end, resolving each gap as you come to it, as follows: Work to 1 st before gap, with right-hand needle lift right leg of st below next st on left-hand needle onto left-hand needle, k2tog (lifted st and the following st).
Resume working in the rnd.

Resolution Rnd 2: Work to end, resolving each gap as you come to it, as follows: Work to gap, with right-hand needle lift right left of st below next st on left-hand needle (the st just after the gap) onto left-hand needle, k2tog (lifted st and the following st).

Shape Yoke

Raglan Increase Rnd: K5, sm, [work to 1 st before marker, M1L, k1, sm, k1, M1R] 4 times, work to end—8 sts increased.
Work 1 rnd even.

Repeat the last 2 rnds 32 (30, 27, 18) (22, 17, 9, 2) more times—343 (327, 307, 239) (275, 239, 179, 127) sts; 5 steek sts, 45 (43, 41, 33) (38, 34, 27, 21) sts each front, 78 (74, 68, 50) (58, 48, 32, 18) sts each sleeve, 92 (88, 84, 68) (78, 70, 56, 44) sts for back.

Repeat Raglan Increase Rnd once.
Work 1 rnd even.

Body Increase Rnd: K5, sm, [work to 1 st before marker, M1L, k1, sm, k1, work to 1 st before next marker, k1, sm, k1, M1R] twice, work to end—4 sts increased.
Work 1 rnd even.

Repeat the last 4 rnds 3 (5, 7, 12) (10, 13, 17, 21) more times—391 (399, 403, 395) (407, 407, 395,

391) sts; 5 steek sts, 53 (55, 57, 59) (60, 62, 63, 65) sts each front, 86 (86, 84, 76) (80, 76, 68, 62) sts each sleeve, 108 (112, 116, 120) (122, 126, 128, 132) sts for back.

Divide for Body and Sleeves

Dividing Rnd: K5, sm, work across left front sts to marker, remove marker, place next 86 (86, 84, 76) (80, 76, 68, 62) sts on holder or waste yarn for left sleeve, remove marker, CO 6 (14, 22, 30) (36, 44, 54, 62) sts for underarm (placing marker at center of CO sts), work across back sts to marker, remove marker, place next 86 (86, 84, 76) (80, 76, 68, 62) sts on holder or waste yarn for right sleeve, remove marker, CO 6 (14, 22, 30) (36, 44, 54, 62) sts for underarm (placing marker at center of CO sts), work to end—231 (255, 279, 303) (319, 343, 367, 391) sts.

BODY

Set-Up Rnd: K5, sm, [work as established to 1 st before marker, k1, sm, k1] twice, work as established to end.

Work even until piece measures 7 (6¾, 6¾, 6¾) (7, 7¼, 7¾, 8)" [18 (17, 17, 17) (18, 18.5, 19.5, 20.5) cm], or to 2¼" (5.5 cm) less than desired length from underarm.

Note: *If you wish to add more Latvian Braids before working the 2×2 Rib, you may adjust the length at this point to accommodate additional braids; each braid will add ¼" (6 cm) in length.*

Knit 1 rnd.

Next Rnd: K1, using 2 colors of your choice, work Left-Leaning Latvian Braid to end.

Work even until braid is complete.

Work Rnds 1–3 of Left-Leaning Latvian Braid once more, then work Rnds 1–3 of Right-Leaning Latvian Braid once.

Next Rnd: K5, sm, k2, *p2, k2; repeat from * to end.

Work even for 1½" (4 cm).

BO all sts using your favorite stretchy BO.

SLEEVES

With RS facing, transfer sleeve sts to needle(s) in your preferred style for working in the rnd.

Rejoin yarn at center underarm; pick up and knit 3 (7, 11, 15) (18, 22, 27, 31) sts from sts CO for underarm, work in pattern as established to end, pick up and knit 3 (7, 11, 15) (18, 22, 27, 31) sts from sts CO for underarm; pm and join for working in the rnd.

Next Rnd: K1, work to last st, k1.

Shape Sleeve

Decrease Rnd: K1, k2tog, work to last 3 sts, ssk, k1—2 sts decreased.

Repeat Decrease Rnd every 6 (6, 4, 4) (4, 4, 4, 4) rnds 5 (1, 26, 28) (25, 23, 24, 24) more time(s), then every 4 (4, 2, 0) (2, 2, 2, 2) rnds 18 (26, 4, 0) (6, 10, 8, 9) times—44 (44, 44, 48) (52, 52, 56, 56) sts remain.

Work even until piece measures 14¼ (15¼, 15½, 15½) (15½, 15½, 15½, 15¾)" [36 (38.5, 39.5, 39.5) (39.5, 39.5, 39.5, 40) cm] from underarm.

Next Rnd: Using 2 colors of your choice, work Left-Leaning Latvian Braid to end.

Work even until braid is complete.

Work Rnds 1–3 of Right-Leaning Latvian Braid once, then work Rnds 1–3 of Left-Leaning Latvian Braid once. Repeat the last 2 braids once more.

Work in Circular 2×2 Rib for 1½" (4 cm).

BO all sts using your favorite stretchy BO.

FINISHING

Close any gaps at the underarms. Soak in warm water until water is cool. Roll piece in towels to press out water, then lay flat to dry, shaping to schematic measurements. Cut the steek according to instructions on page 125.

Turn the raw edge of one steek to the WS of the front. Using a tapestry needle and some waste yarn from your project, seam the edge securely to the inside of the garment. You can hide any ends for the Latvian Braids in this section as well.

Carefully unpick your steek stabilizing crochet chains and use an iron on the highest steam setting to gently press these fronts flat for easy stitch pick up.

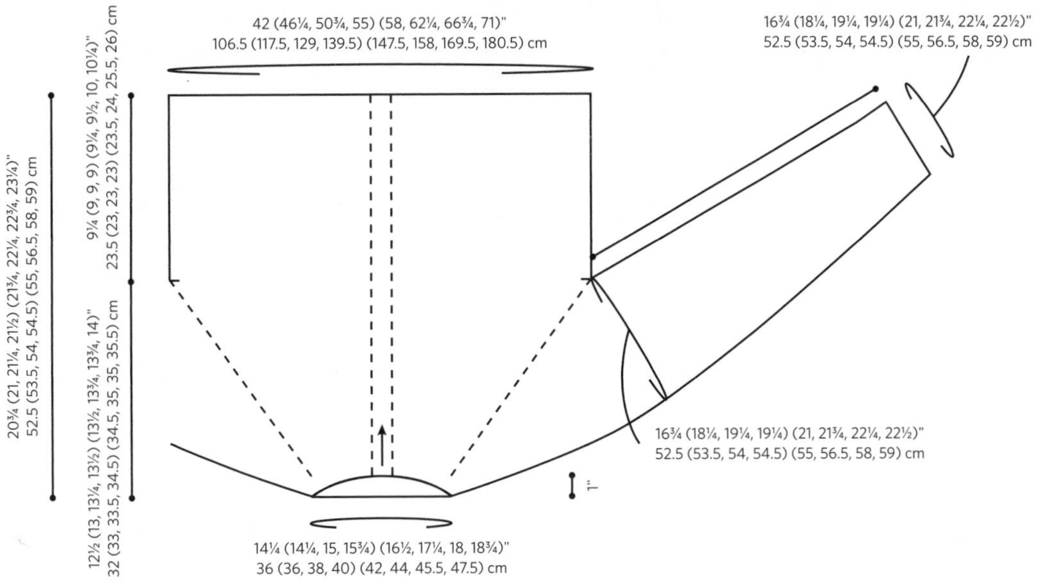

20¾ (21, 21¼, 21½) (21¾, 22¼, 22¾, 23¼)"
52.5 (53.5, 54, 54.5) (55, 56.5, 58, 59) cm
9¼ (9, 9, 9) (9¼, 9½, 10, 10¼)"
23.5 (23, 23, 23) (23.5, 24, 25.5, 26) cm
12½ (13, 13¼, 13½) (13½, 13¾, 13¾, 14)"
32 (33, 33.5, 34.5) (34.5, 35, 35, 35.5) cm
42 (46¼, 50¾, 55) (58, 62¼, 66¾, 71)"
106.5 (117.5, 129, 139.5) (147.5, 158, 169.5, 180.5) cm
16¾ (18¼, 19¼, 19¼) (21, 21¾, 22¼, 22½)"
52.5 (53.5, 54, 54.5) (55, 56.5, 58, 59) cm
16¾ (18¼, 19¼, 19¼) (21, 21¾, 22¼, 22½)"
52.5 (53.5, 54, 54.5) (55, 56.5, 58, 59) cm
1"
14¼ (14¼, 15, 15¾) (16½, 17¼, 18, 18¾)"
36 (36, 38, 40) (42, 44, 45.5, 47.5) cm

Note: *Pieces are worked from the top down. The neck and bust meeasurements are before cutting the steek and working the front bands.*

Button Band

With RS facing, using circular needle and beginning at left neck edge, pick up and knit 108 (112, 112, 112) (116, 116, 120, 124) sts along left front.

Begin Flat 2×2 Rib, beginning with a WS row; work even until piece measures 1½" (4 cm) from pick-up row, ending with a WS row.

BO all sts using your favorite stretchy BO.

Place removable markers to mark position of buttons, the top button aligned with the neck braid, the bottom button at the base of the bottom braid, and the remaining 4 buttons evenly spaced between.

Buttonhole Band

With RS facing, using circular needle and beginning at lower right front edge, pick up and knit 108 (112, 112, 112) (116, 116, 120, 124) sts along right front.

Begin Flat 2×2 Rib, beginning with a WS row; work even until piece measures ½" (1.3 cm) from pickup row, ending with a WS row. Place removable markers to correspond to markers on left front.

Buttonhole Row 1 (RS): [Work to 1 st before marker, BO 2 sts (removing marker)] 6 times, work to end.

Buttonhole Row 2: [Work to buttonhole, CO 2 sts] 6 times, work to end.

Work even until piece measures 1½" (4 cm) from pick-up row, ending with a WS row.

BO all sts using your favorite stretchy BO.

Wet block piece again if desired. Sew buttons at markers.

Sewing On Sturdy Buttons

Sewing on a sturdy button is an essential step in any cardigan project, and learning how to sew on buttons properly was one of my favorite things in fashion school. It's such a necessary skill that, surprisingly, few people know how to do. To sew a button onto a knitted project might seem daunting at first, but I promise, it's quite easy. There are a few considerations that you should make about your buttons and the yarn or thread you choose to sew them on with.

First, decide if you are going to be matching the thread to the buttons or to the garment. This little decision can make a statement on your garment, so be sure to think about it and find yarn or thread that matches your vision of the finished piece. Choosing between thread and yarn is fairly straightforward: If the yarn is too thick for the buttonholes or the needle, switch over to a thread or smaller yarn that matches the buttons or garment. If the yarn is delicate, like single ply or carded, woolen-spun yarn, consider switching to a stronger thread, like embroidery or Pearl Cotton, which has a nice sheen to it and always looks crisp.

Pull out about 1 yard (.9 m) of thread or yarn. If using thread, thread the needle and pull the ends together, tying a slipknot so your needle is on a single, circular loop of thread. This essentially doubles up your thread and makes it a little thicker, and therefore less likely to cut through your yarn over time. If using a single strand of a strong yarn, thread the needle and do not tie the ends, instead pulling one end of the yarn much longer than the other.

Pull your yarn or thread through the back of the fabric. If using a single loop, go back through on the next column of stitches and catch the loop with your needle on the same side as the knot, bringing the knot up next to the fabric and securing it.

If using the single strand, leave a short tail (about 3" [7.5 cm]) on the reverse side. You will need to take care to secure it with your fingers for the first few steps with the button, but this is easy enough to do with a little practice (after all, you do the same tensioning when you knit).

Next, we'll attach the button. The button I'm using has two holes, so I don't have many options for stitch patterns: My stitches will just be a bar. If you're using a button with four or more holes, consider what sort of "weaving" pattern you want to use for your button. Look some up online—you'll be amazed by the cleverness people have regarding button attachment!

The key to making a button look nice and clean on a knitted fabric is to be careful to go in between the stitch columns evenly, and not to

pierce the knitted strands (which causes them to fray and can make your button look saggy). Come back up and through the opposite side cleanly each time and your button will look crisp and straight. Go through the button in the intended pattern of holes several times to create a secure bundle of thread.

When you feel that your button is sturdy, bring the needle up through the button as normal, but come only through the button—not the fabric—on the reverse side.

Wrap the remaining thread or yarn tightly around the base of the button to create a shank. A shank helps your shankless (flat) buttons attach to the fabric but stand out from it a little, so that the pull of using the buttons is mainly on the thread and not on your knitted fabric.

Note: when you use a shank button, you simply make the loops and then secure it on the back.

Bring the needle back up through the back of the button and then down through the top, but as you come through the top of the button, try to push the needle's tip down into the shank as you bring it through to the back of the fabric. If this step feels too tight, be careful and use a thimble to avoid piercing your fingers!

Bring the thread back through itself on the back side of the fabric, tying it into a secure knot and clipping off any extra. Save a little of your button thread match for later, and keep it with your darning yarns.

THE SACREDNESS
OF TEA AND KNITTING

THE COMBINATION OF TEA AND knitting seems to take me through each day and into the next. I cannot imagine one without the other, especially as the golden, chilly mornings of autumn become steadily more frosty, the grass and every surface coated in crystals that melt off as the sun hits them: a promise of winter closing in.

In the morning, I have found ritual in the pouring of a morning cup. I begin with a favorite mug: It's hand-thrown, the smooth cobalt glaze expertly applied over the slightly warbled surface of pottery. I dip a spoon generously into the jar of honey that sits beside my tea station, and pour a bit of steaming water from the kettle into the cup, the rolling boil just fading out of it. Swirling the spoon, I make my morning tea selection: Earl Grey, rich in tannins and bergamot; or English breakfast, a classic accompaniment for scones or toast. Black tea in the morning gets me going and is the perfect companion for bird watching, chores around the house, or a bit of reading beneath the covers on the weekends. Of course, tea is always welcome where knitting is involved, too.

Tea has become almost ubiquitous in our craft. Perhaps it's the long history of humans and tea that has led to the association, but I think it's more likely that the beverage and the practice of drinking it have become so similar to knitting that they simply must go hand in hand. Black leaves or green, tea brings warmth and coziness to knitting moments alone or with friends. There is nothing quite so charming as the round bubble of a teapot, wrapped in its own wool sweater; and nothing as welcoming to visitors as being poured a cup of something steaming and offered a bowl of sugar cubes.

I have longed to have a space appropriate for hosting afternoon tea and crafting parties. When I was in my teens, my younger sister sweetly indulged me, buying the perfect, orchid-pink tea set, complete with delicate cream pitcher and cheery sugar bowl. Each part of the set is round and pleasing, and over time I have managed to pair them with enamel-painted,

Japanese porcelain cups procured from online vintage shops. When I bring them out for visitors, it makes the time together feel exceptional, and planned. With a teacup in hand, we can feel instantly at home in a space that is not our own.

Tea, like knitting, teaches us patience and anticipation. Every tea variety requires us to spend some time researching and experimenting to find the perfect balance of bitter tannin and steeping time; the right balance of sugar or honey to bring the flavors out rather than hide them. Whether we have to wait three minutes or twelve, we spend this time taking a moment to process,

to contemplate, and to slow down. The discipline we practice here echoes the discipline required to complete a knitting project, and the acceptance that the things we desire take time, and that the time involved is part of the process.

Likewise, the care with which we select tea and the preferences we develop seem to be reflected in our process of curating a knitting stash. Over the past year, a good friend has shared the secrets of tea with me, and I the secrets of selecting wools and projects with her. Through this mutual exchange, we've both developed and discovered preferences. It's funny how so many things in our lives reflect others, and I feel that my favorite selections of tea can be matched to the colors in my stash.

I have developed a love for wax-wrapped cakes of fermented pu-erh, which can be broken and then steeped. The leaves unfurl gently in hot water and release a tannin-rich, deep amber tea. I see this love for aged color in my knitting, too: Deep oxbloods and warm golden browns have begun to line my shelves and adorn my needles.

Other days, I crave the smoky, mellow taste of a lapsang souchong, which I first discovered through a journey to Charleston, South Carolina, and the purchase of Colonial Bohea. It's an eggcorn name, a mispronunciation of Wuyi, the name of the mountain range in China from which this tea comes. These tea leaves smell strong in the bag, like a campfire, and remind me of faded jeans and deep indigo blues.

Pale creams and foggy, misty grays have made their way into my yarns, and I find similar tones in each early morning cup of Earl Grey. These are familiar, easy-to-wear hues: They go with everything, and every moment is for them. The same can be said, at least in my experience, of the classic bergamot scent of this black tea, which I couple with local honey and a splash of oat milk. They are no-frills, but just right.

When I'm feeling busy and bright, the sharpness of matcha or gunpowder green tea, cut with a bit of honey, restores my focus. I find myself most drawn to acidic yellows and citrons during these moments, the bright colors tempered by a touch of darkness that pulls them back from neon to natural.

I wonder, sometimes, if this phenomenon extends to other knitters, and encourage you to see where your stash matches your teas, if you are a tea drinker: Do those who prefer the sweetness of fruity flavored teas gravitate toward bright jewel tones or vivid indie dyes? Are you strict English breakfast drinkers also fans of a good workhorse yarn in classic shades? Do our preferences here overlap and influence each other, or are these simply projections that I've cast on my own habits?

These are things to contemplate, of course, over a cup of something hot.

pampering yourself

Fall is a time for slowing down and preparing. We're focused on all the days ahead that we'll spend indoors, so trying to get outside while the weather is still nice—and complete every chore that seems to be hanging over our heads—can have us feeling extra frenzied. In between filling the bird feeder, winterizing the garden, dumping out (and cleaning) flowerpots, I encourage you to take a little more time to take care of yourself, too.

TAKE A BATH

It sounds so simple in theory: Fill the tub with water and get into it. There are so many additional options for dressing up time in hot water. If your skin will handle them, bath bombs are available in almost any scent, color, and effect. For those of us who need something a little more old-fashioned to unwind, I love adding a few drops of moisturizing oil or Epsom salts to the bathtub before climbing in. A bath is time away from the world, in the privacy of a space you've created, so take advantage of it. Light candles, play relaxing music, or simply sit in the silence and breathe in some good old-fashioned aromatherapy.

READ A BOOK

While you can certainly add this activity to one of the others, I find that getting away to read something purely fun or interesting for an hour (or two) can be the perfect reset I need. If you have a busy or noisy home life, see if you can escape to a cozy café with a cup of coffee. If your personal time is mostly late in the evening, an hour of reading is better for your brain than screen time, so set down the phone and computer, turn off the TV, and flip some pages.

PAMPER YOUR SKIN

Skin care has become one of my favorite nightly rituals: I have a process I work through each night, step by step, and the results, while slow (it takes two weeks for your skin to catch up to whatever you've applied), are well worth any time spent on them. Once a week, I spend an hour on more in-depth skin care treatments like facials or masks.

GET A MASSAGE

I hate scheduling massages. They seem so expensive and inconvenient: I have to make an appointment, I have to keep it, and I have to have the funds to pay a dollar a minute (or more) for someone to work on me and my needs. When I lay on the table, though, and fully relax while my masseuse works out my tired muscles and sore spots, it all seems worth it. Massage is good for us in so many ways, and the results are reflected almost instantly in the way we move and feel.

TEA BLENDS FOR KNITTING

RUSSIAN CARAVAN
(FROM CHURCHMOUSE YARNS & TEAS)

A dark blend of oolong, keemun, and lapsang souchong tea, this smoky-tasting black tea is one of my favorites for early morning knitting, and gains new depth when blended with a bit of oat milk and honey. This is a smooth tea that pairs well with Stockinette stitch and an audiobook. Another favorite smoky black tea is Colonial Bohea, also known as Bohea Souchong or Lapsang Bohea. Oddly enough, this colonial tea used to be made from scrap tea leaves and could have a massive variation in blend; my favorite is offered by US producer Oliver Pluff & Co.

DRAGONWELL GREEN TEA NO. 30
(FROM TEA CHAI TÉ)

This bright, flat-leafed tea comes to us directly from Hangzhou, China, and is considered one of the world's finest green teas. I drink my green tea unsweetened and love this as a midafternoon pick-me-up when I'm working with numbers and complex patterns. Save this caffeinated, fresh tea for working lace or similarly intricate techniques like brioche, entrelac, or colorwork. Another favorite in this category is Gunpowder green tea, also offered via Oliver Pluff & Co.

BUTTER BREW
(FROM BIRD & BLEND TEA CO.)

Flavored teas seem to be a favorite of many drinkers in America. Whether we're mixing in fruit flavors like white peach or passion fruit, or adding warmer flavors to the mix like caramel, cinnamon, or nutmeg, there are endless varieties of flavored tea available. I love to pair these "treat" teas with equally rewarding knitting projects: something soft and easy to work on. This Butter Brew blend mimics the Butterbeer in *Harry Potter* tales and is delicious hot, but I also love fruit, floral, and flavored tea blends iced. Looking for another variety to try? I also enjoy Ahmad Tea's Peach & Passion Fruit.

CEYLON ORANGE PEKOE
(FROM CHURCHMOUSE YARNS & TEAS)

This lovely traditional tea is a bit floral and bitter, but a few sugar cubes or a dash of honey makes it one of my go-to favorites for knitting any time of day. It's a go-to tea for your go-to project, whether that means a sweater, socks, or a shawl. If you love Earl Grey or English breakfast, this tea will line up perfectly with your other favorites in the tea cabinet.

Homemade Body Oil

A few years ago, I discovered a must-have body product. As a girl with extremely dry skin that soaks up lotion like a sponge, I was going through even the thickest, most luxurious body creams at a prodigious speed each autumn and winter. Somewhere along the way, I read an article about body oils, and tried some store-bought ones before deciding that it might be infinitely more affordable—and customizable—to make my own. The process of making your own body oil is easy.

First, you'll need a base or carrier oil. This oil is going to make up most of your blend, so it's important to choose one or two that are affordable and moisturizing. Look for oils not in the food section of the grocery store but in the beauty section of your local co-op: They'll be more refined and of better quality. After you know what oil blend is best for you, it's also possible to order in bulk online for better pricing. My favorite carrier oil is grapeseed oil, but I have also tried (and loved) avocado oil, shea butter oil, and safflower oil. Look for an oil that isn't too thick, so that it goes on as a smooth and light layer. You'll want to use carrier oils for about 70 percent of your blend.

Then, find a supplemental liquid to add to your carrier. As a knitter, I love to use lanolin. Liquid lanolin is a byproduct of our wool industry and has become a great additional source of income for mills and scouring plants. It's amber in color and a bit sticky as-is, so you can use it sparingly for about 25 percent of your final blend. Other great add-ins include more luxurious, and expensive, oils: rose hip seed oil, jojoba oil, and marula oil are wonderful to add to your blend. Lanolin is excellent for skin that easily chaps or chafes, while rose hip seed oil fights breakouts and marula is gentle for sensitive skin. You can mix more than one of these additions into your blend for great results. Put them in a bowl and whisk or stir them together to blend.

The last 5 percent of your body oil blend is scent. If you'd like to leave it unscented, you can skip this bit, but I like to add a little scent to my body oils to help the experience of using them feel extraspecial. You can infuse your carrier oil with scents by letting herbs or whole spices (like anise or vanilla) soak in a bottle of the carrier oil for a few months—or simplify the process and use essential oils with scents you love.

You'll need more scent than you initially think when using essential oils, but it's easier to add more than to take away. Add some drops to your carrier and supplemental mix, then rub a bit into your skin to see how the scent reacts with your skin or fades over time. I usually start with a teaspoon of scent and go from there.

Pour your body oil into a dark-colored bottle with a dropper or pump: This is the easiest way to apply your oil and much simpler than attempting to dip or pour amounts out in your palm each time you use it. Apply the oil to your skin right after drying off from a shower or bath to seal in the remaining moisture.

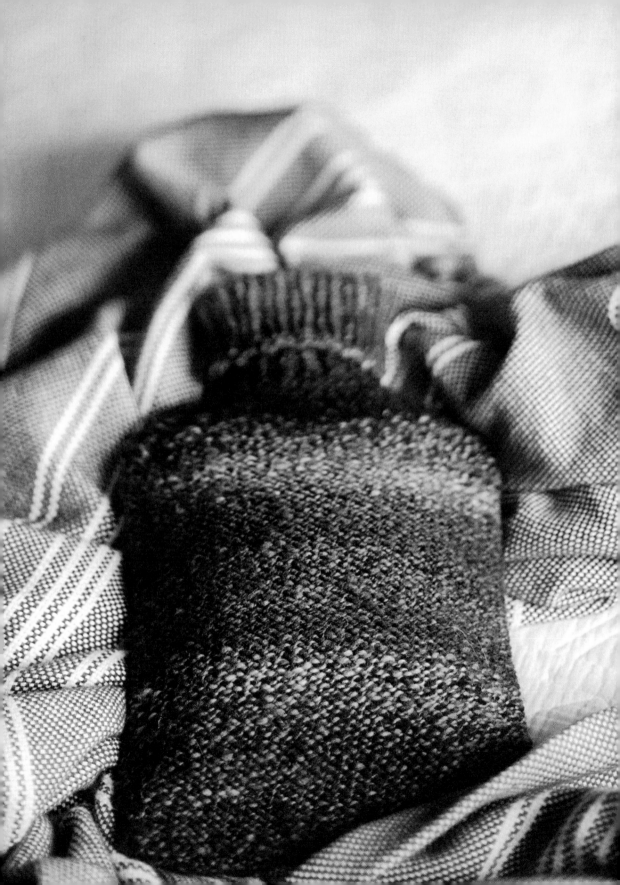

Thusa Cozy

/ *About the Yarn* /

HELLO YARN FIBER: WORSTED-WEIGHT HANDSPUN

I have been buying Adrian Bizilia's handspun for almost a decade now. I have had not only the pleasure of purchasing from Adrian but also the opportunity to see her color genius in action, through occasional attendance at Yarn School, in picturesque Harveyville, Kansas, by Nikol Lohr. Each year, Adrian comes to this (not fully) converted high school, where Nikol hosts low-key teaching retreats for adventurous students hoping to dig deep into spinning, dyeing, weaving, mitten making, baking, brewing, cheese making, and more. The setting is funky and fun, with a bit of a lock-in vibe, and the school has become a well-kept secret, attended by devoted returnees.

Adrian's background in the fine arts has set her apart from many indie dyers in the industry, and her brilliance in showcasing color resonates with my deep love of it. A little grunginess as a background for brilliant color is her hallmark: A bit of yellowy green or muddled burgundy-brown gives way to brilliant oranges, pinks, violets, and blues. Above all, she is firmly aware of her unique canvas, wool, down to the specific breed. How each wool takes color has become something of an ongoing experiment for Adrian and for those who purchase her club and shop offerings.

You see, spinners know a secret. If you can get someone to spend enough time marveling at making wool into yarn that can become a garment, they're going to love whatever results from their spinning endeavors. They will cherish that first, wobbly skein of handspun as if it was the most precious of children, because they have slipped every bit between their fingers and watched it become. This feeling is so deeply rewarding that they ache to complete the action again and watch the process. Add soul-satisfying color that transforms and transitions on the wheel, and you're gone—you're into the business of spinning hook, line, and sinker.

SIZE

Designed to fit a hot-water bottle 8½" (21 cm) wide by 10½" (26.5 cm) long from bottom to base of neck, with a neck height of 2½" (6 cm) and a neck circumference of 7½" (19 cm).

FINISHED MEASUREMENTS

16" (40.5 cm) circumference by 9½" (24 cm) from base to beginning of "shoulders"

YARN

Hello Yarn Fiber worsted-weight handspun, spun by me

ALTERNATIVE YARNS

200 yards (183 meters) of worsted-weight wool
For that brilliantly wooly, beaded effect, nothing but handspun will do. Look for hand-spinners in your country and choose something someone made right around the corner from your home. Alternatively, you can learn to spin.

NEEDLES

Size US 8 (5 mm) needle(s) in your preferred style for working in the rnd

Change needle size if necessary to obtain correct gauge.

NOTIONS

Stitch markers

GAUGE

15½ sts and 24 rnds = 4" (10 cm) in St st

PATTERN NOTES

I named this little hot-water bottle cozy after my cat, Thusa. The first animal I welcomed into my life while living on my own, this sweet little cat has been through it all, and holds my heart so close to hers. I delight every time she wants to snuggle up in winter (her coat keeps her warm except on the chilliest days) and nothing seemed to embody her better than the ultimate cozy making project.

The bottle cozy is worked in the round from the bottom up, then the "shoulders" are shaped and the neck is worked. The piece is worked with the knit side facing for ease of knitting, but shown with the purl side facing; you may use either side as the right side.

After the cozy is complete, the bottom is sewn closed, with the hot water bottle inside. The bottle I used is sold by a company called HomeTop. It is made from rubber and has a screw stopper. It is possible to modify your cozy to fit any size or shape.

COZY

Note: Use your preferred method of working in the rnd.

CO 62 sts. Join for working in the rnd, being careful not to twist sts; pm for beginning of rnd. Begin St st (knit every rnd); work even until piece matches the straight length of your bottle, from the bottom to the "shoulders," where the sides curve toward the neck.

Shape Shoulders

Decrease Rnd: K1, pm, ssk, k25, k2tog, pm, k2, pm, ssk, k25, k2tog, k1—4 sts decreased.
Repeat Decrease Rnd every other rnd 5 more times—38 sts remain.
Knit 1 rnd.

Next Rnd: *K2, p2; repeat from * to end.
Work even for 5" (12.5 cm), or until neck is long enough to cover the mouth of your bottle when folded over.
BO all sts in pattern.

FINISHING

Turn Cozy inside out so purl side is facing (or leave knit side facing, if you prefer). Insert bottle into Cozy. Sew bottom opening closed.

LAST LEAVINGS

IT CAN'T BE COINCIDENTAL THAT the two transitional seasons of the year, spring and autumn, are also the showiest. For our environment to shift and change around us is always a humbling experience; to watch nature transform before our eyes in a tangible, evident way, from the blossoming of a new flower to the slow fade of leaves from green to gold. This year, I feel almost as if I've been chasing autumn. In Tennessee, the fatigue of a too-long summer hits me in late September and early October, when the temperatures stubbornly stay around 85°F (29°C) and refuse to dip down for any reprieve. Sweltering and miserable, I spend time gazing longingly at my pile of handknits, wishing I could swap them out and wear something new, begging the weather to change so that I can get out of the pieces I've had in rotation since May.

Thankfully, mid-October is Rhinebeck season, and I am usually able to escape the southern heat and retreat to upstate New York and my beloved New England. The Hudson Valley at this time of year is spectacular, the leaves swinging into brilliant shades of marigold, vermilion, and copper. The air feels crisp and cool, like the crunch of a freshly picked apple; the nights are perfect for cozying up and occasionally even allow for the luxury of a crackling fire. This time away has become crucial for me, and this year I extended it for a journey through Vermont and New Hampshire, ending with a foray along Maine's southern coast. As I traveled, I saw trees and brush in various shades of change, in colors that astounded and excited me. I could wear this palette year-round: chartreuse and ruddy blush, cognac and deep wine, sandy tans and warm golds, set against a sky dappled with sunlight and puffy clouds.

Returning home on Samhain, a Gaelic festival that marks the beginning of winter, I found that Tennessee, too, had been graced with autumn: the leaves were just beginning to show a tinge of yellow on the edges; more importantly, the heat had finally broken, making way for cool nights and glittering, frosty mornings. I was finally able to wrap up in a blanket to knit and bury myself in quilts to sleep. The world feels somehow more right in autumn, and we celebrate it, knowing that this time is short and will soon change over: Two days after I left the Northeast, it snowed there.

Autumn is a held breath that soon changes to a deep, resigned sigh as the weather turns colder and the world settles into hibernation. Blink and the golden, magical season is gone, replaced by lavender skies and fierce winds.

Why are these short periods of transition so appealing to us humans? Perhaps it's their ephemeral nature: Their sudden appearance and subsequent fade reminds us that all things are temporary, that we should make the most of every moment we have and celebrate it for what it brings. At the end of autumn where I live, the leaves fade and fall, brown and curled, soon to be outlined with morning frosts. In the meantime, we grip these golden days tightly, intending to carry them with us into the coming cold.

When we begin to think about it more deeply, each shearing seems like a transitional season: a moment in time, a day in the life of a fiber animal, captured and held through the fluffy curls of wool. In the smell of lanolin, I find the scent of a long winter and brilliant spring, the excitement of the move from one season to the next. In the hand of a spun yarn, I feel the patience, the deliberate, slow movement of a long summer. In the knitting, I find autumn: the knowledge that as our piece grows, the time that we have with it is also passing, fading, moving into something new. A sweater, a shawl, socks, or a hat—each item is a slow metamorphosis from fleece to skein to garment, and we intend to wrap it around us, the way we do autumn's golden days, and carry it into winter.

winter solstice

FIRST FROST

WE HUMANS ARE CERTAINLY FUNNY creatures, apt to pine for that which isn't present, only to want the complete opposite when the object of our desire arrives. Such is my relationship with the changing of each season, especially now that I've experienced what it's like to live in multiple places. As a child, I lived in the southeastern United States almost exclusively. Winter, to my elementary-school-aged self, meant a period of time in Atlanta when you could see your breath in the air. When we moved to Kentucky, I saw the magic of a hoarfrost for the first time: low fog, frozen directly onto every surface of the world in sharp, thin layers of crystalline ice.

My sister and I would stand eagerly at the glass front door, waiting for the school bus to show up over the long hill, and then run out to wait, shivering for the few moments it took for it to stop. The horses in the pastures beyond, their borders outlined by fences painted black with pitch, didn't seem to mind the cold. They stood hoof-deep in the inches of crunchy snow and snorted thick, hot clouds of breath into the air, tails swishing. I watched them from the bus window every morning as we rode away.

When I was eleven, we moved from Kentucky a little farther north, to central Virginia. Here, we would get little snows that made the county close schools, and kids in the neighborhood would sneak onto the nearby golf course and attempt to sled down the hills (mainly just ruining the grass). It got cold sometimes, but it wasn't the cold I would feel when we moved to Iowa in my late teens.

Iowa is a midwestern state with rolling hills that are occupied by corn and soybeans all summer long. You can watch a breeze come by and rustle the stalks of corn in emerald-green waves that shine in the hot sun. In the winter, these plains are barren, the harvest cut down by combines, and all that remains are short, dried stalks, broken off a few inches up and churned back into the dark soil. These catch and gather the snow.

The first year we lived in Iowa, I was shocked by the snow. I had dreamed of a snowy, white holiday season when I was small. What child hasn't seen movies that showcase the magic of snow in December? In Iowa, it really doesn't typically snow in December. January, February, and March are snow months—and when it snows, it snows deep, heavy drifts that bury your car and hide the mailbox. It snows continuously for hours, so you begin your shoveling early in the hope that there might be only a few inches and you can get out and go to work. It snows and then the snow packs down on top of other snow, forming a thick layer that acts like ice in patches.

Then there is the cold. True winter cold is a deep cold. It hits you with the first outdoor breath, your first inhalation freezing the inside of your nose and making your eyes water. The cold is bone-deep and vicious, reminding you that you're currently alive but making mortality a tangible feeling. In some Iowa winters, news channels warn against going outside with any part of your face showing for more than a few moments. That first winter, we wrapped our thin, useless scarves around our necks and stuffed fingers into dollar store–bought gloves. I was a knitter, but I had never experienced this level of cold, and I realized that the craft I had been practicing had deeper

purpose now, in the Midwest, than it ever had before.

If my childhood in Kentucky led to my learning how to knit, it was my time in Iowa that honed and molded my passion for knitting. There is something magical about casting on an item you know you will use over and over, every day for several months. Planning what scarf will go with your coat, or knitting a sweater you can imagine curling up in, is something every knitter should have the opportunity to experience. It's why I have become such an advocate of knitting to fit your wardrobe, rather than knitting what is popular. Knitting what you will wear is the most rewarding way to knit.

Winter knitting in Tennessee doesn't give me the same thrill as binding off a pattern in Iowa did, but I do appreciate the lack of wind that howls and beats against you. The wind in Iowa is punishing, with temperatures that drop far into the negative and extend seemingly forever into spring. In Tennessee, we might have only a few days a year that drop below freezing, and most of my sweater wearing is done without a coat.

But still, when those first few chilly mornings arrive and I can see frost on the grass, some part of my knitting heart is reminded, and filled with the anticipation of a purpose for my woolens. This is the magic of the first frost.

Coffee Hour Pullover

/ *About the Yarn* /

PEACE FLEECE DK

In Iowa, it was an absolute necessity to have more than one warm woolen sweater, like a pullover you could layer over silk underwear and a long-sleeved T-shirt, an insulating buffer to make you more comfortable on windy, icy days. In Tennessee, these trusty layers find wear only in the deepest months of our Southern winters. I have found, though, that I still reach for my favorite wool pullovers frequently, as if they were sweatshirts, tossing them on for a quick trip to the store, or cozying up at home while writing and knitting. While I certainly need fewer warm sweaters, I wanted to create one that would have a polished, structured look, and found myself inspired by recent runway knits that feature fabrics like neoprene. I've replaced these bulky scuba fabrics with beloved heathered Peace Fleece in Stockinette and Linen Stitch, and paired it with an easy-to-understand shape that knitters of all skill levels can embrace.

Since the 1970s, Peace Fleece has been produced through a shared love of wool and raising sheep. Originally, the blended fibers came from Russia, Kyrgyzstan, Ukraine, and Israel, and were combined with wool from Cottage Hill Farm in Ohio, and mohair from ranches in Texas. In 2008, the founder's son, Silas, participated in the filming of a horseback ride with the Lakota and Dakota tribes to honor a great tragedy—the 1863 mass execution of forty tribal leaders and members. The trip brought home a point to Silas that there was as much work to be done to heal relationships within the United States. He pushed for Peace Fleece to become a part of this process, transitioning to collaborations with the Navajo Nation in the American Southwest. Now, Peace Fleece's wool is sourced domestically, and the percentage of Navajo ranchers involved increases year after year.

Peace Fleece is now dyed and milled at the Harrisville Mill in New Hampshire. Each colorway is a blend of many different colors, hand-selected and then carded by practiced artisans. The yarn is distributed around the world, and each purchase directly benefits the Navajo Nation, in an effort to build new connections for the future.

SIZES

To fit bust sizes 32–34 (36–38, 40–42, 44–46) (48–50, 52–54, 56–58, 60–62)" [81.5–86.5 (91.5–96.5, 101.5–106.5, 112–117) (122–127, 132–137, 142–147.5, 152.5–157.5) cm]

FINISHED MEASUREMENTS

41¾ (46¼, 49¼, 53¾) (58¼, 62¼, 66¼, 69¼)" [106 (117.5, 125, 136.5) (148, 158, 168.5, 176) cm] bust

YARN

Peace Fleece DK [75% Rambouillet, 25% mohair, domestically grown, dyed and milled; 350 yards (320 meters)/4 ounces (114 grams)]: 5 (6, 6, 6) (7, 8, 8, 8) skeins Mourning Dove

ALTERNATIVE YARNS

1,690 (1,880, 1,960, 2,110) (2,300, 2,515, 2,670, 2,805) yards [1,547 (1,720, 1,792, 1,932) (2,102, 2,299, 2,442, 2,564) meters] in a worsted-weight yarn

Calling this yarn a DK weight might be a stretch. In the skein and on the needles, this Peace Fleece performs beautifully at worsted-weight gauges and works up quickly and effortlessly on larger needles. This gives you plenty of time to admire the beautifully heathered, complex colors that make up a single skein. Mourning Dove, the color I've chosen, appears to be faded, rusty red at first glance, but look closer and you'll discover little flecks of orange, pink, red, and black. If you'd like to substitute another yarn, look for a true worsted weight with a hearty hand that adds a bit of stiffness to the Linen Stitch collar and cuffs.

(Canada) Briggs & Little Heritage (100% wool)

(Japan) Noro Kureyon (100% wool)

(UK) Blacker Yarns British Classic Aran Knitting Yarn (100% British wool)

NEEDLES

Size US 8 (5 mm) circular needle 32" (80 cm) long and needle(s) in your preferred style for working in the rnd

Change needle size if necessary to obtain correct gauge.

NOTIONS

Stitch markers, including 1 in a unique style or color for beginning of rnd; stitch holders or waste yarn

GAUGE

14 sts and 20 rows = 4" (10 cm) in St st, wet-blocked
20 sts and 32 rows = 4" (10 cm in Linen Stitch: 5 sts × 8 rounds = 1" (2.5 cm)/20 × 32 rounds = 4" (10 cm), wet-blocked

STITCH PATTERN
CIRCULAR LINEN STITCH
(even number of sts; 2-rnd repeat)
Rnd 1: *K1, slip 1 wyif; repeat from * to last 2 sts, k1, k1-tbl.
Rnd 2: *Slip 1 wyif, k1; repeat from * to last 2 sts, slip 1 wyif, k1-tbl.
Repeat Rnds 1 and 2 for Circular Linen Stitch.

FLAT LINEN STITCH
(odd number of st; 2-row repeat)
Row 1 (RS): K1, *slip 1 wyif, k1; repeat from * to end.
Row 2: Slip 1 wyib, *p1, slip 1 wyib; repeat from * to end.
Repeat Rows 1 and 2 for Flat Linen Stitch.

PATTERN NOTES

This sweater is knit top-down, beginning with the sturdy funnel neckline and moving into a very standard yoke construction. It is worked in the round, split for the sleeves, and then worked from the underarm down in the round before splitting at the hem for a comfortable tent shape. The tapered arms are then finished with Linen Stitch on the cuffs. Please note that the Linen Stitch sections do not have significant stretch, so if your wrist size is a bit larger than indicated on the schematic or you would like more room at the cuff (the ease is about 1½" [4 cm]), end your decreases earlier to achieve a wider cuff.

BEGINNING MEDITATIONS

This pattern uses a form of Linen Stitch that features a very pretty faux seam at the back of the neck. I recommend working this section of the sweater in Magic Loop for simplicity, but you're welcome to tackle it with double points if you feel so inclined.

COLLAR

Using needle(s) in your preferred style for working in the rnd and the Long-Tail CO (see Special Techniques, page 188), CO 111 (111, 111, 121) (121, 127, 127, 127) sts. Join for working in the rnd, being careful not to twist sts; pm in unique style or color for beginning of rnd. *Note: Beginning of rnd is at center back.*

Begin Circular Linen Stitch; work even until piece measures 3" (7.5 cm) or desired length from the beginning.

YOKE

Next Rnd: K2tog, knit to end—110 (110, 110, 120) (120, 126, 126, 126) sts remain.

Set-Up Rnd: *K11 (11, 11, 10) (10, 9, 9, 9), pm; repeat from * to end, omitting last marker. You now have 10 (10, 10, 12) (12, 14, 14, 14) markers, including the beginning-of-rnd marker.

Shape Yoke

Increase Rnd: *Knit to marker, M1L; repeat from * to end—10 (10, 10, 12) (12, 14, 14, 14) sts increased.

Repeat Increase Rnd every 4 (4, 2, 4) (4, 4, 4, 2) rnds 8 (12, 1, 8) (14, 10, 13, 1) more time(s), then every 6 (6, 4, 6) (6, 6, 6, 4) rnds 3 (1, 13, 4) (0, 3, 1, 14) time(s)—230 (250, 260, 276) (300, 322, 336, 350) sts.

Knit 1 rnd, removing all but beginning-of-rnd marker.

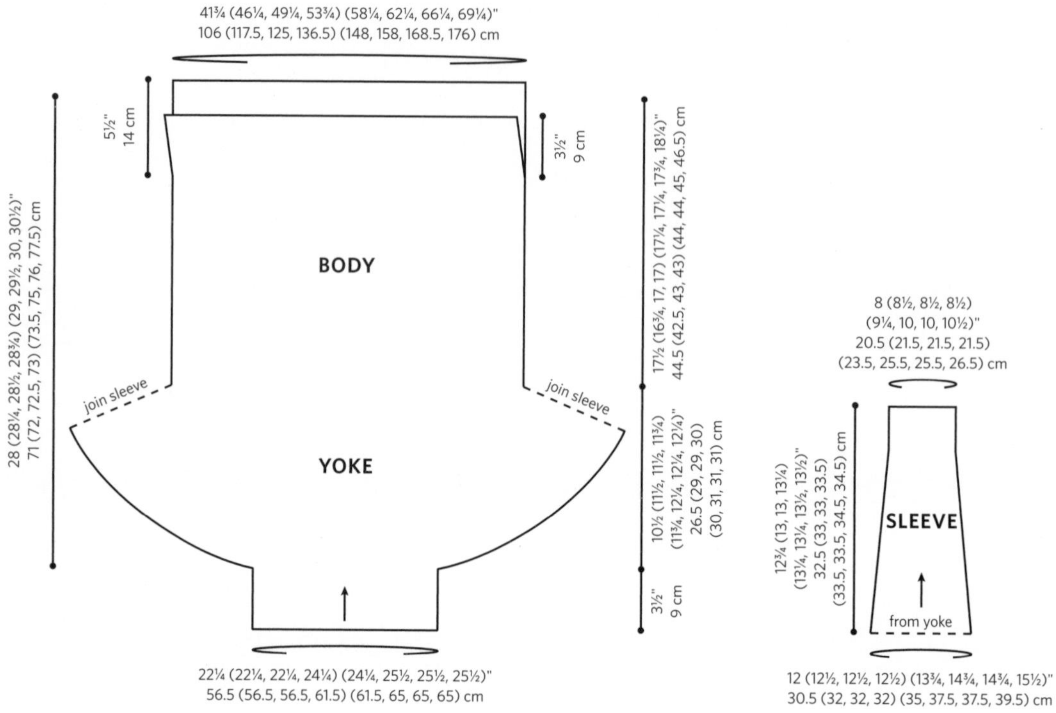

41¾ (46¼, 49¼, 53¾) (58¼, 62¼, 66¼, 69¼)"
106 (117.5, 125, 136.5) (148, 158, 168.5, 176) cm
5½"
14 cm
3½"
9 cm
28 (28¼, 28½, 28¾) (29, 29½, 30, 30½)"
71 (72, 72.5, 73) (73.5, 75, 76, 77.5) cm
BODY
17½ (16¾, 17, 17) (17¼, 17¼, 17¾, 18¼)"
44.5 (42.5, 43, 43) (44, 44, 45, 46.5) cm
join sleeve
join sleeve
YOKE
10½ (11½, 11½, 11¾)
(11¾, 12¼, 12¼, 12¼)"
26.5 (29, 29, 30)
(30, 31, 31, 31) cm
3½"
9 cm
22¼ (22¼, 22¼, 24¼) (24¼, 25½, 25½, 25½)"
56.5 (56.5, 56.5, 61.5) (61.5, 65, 65, 65) cm
8 (8½, 8½, 8½)
(9¼, 10, 10, 10½)"
20.5 (21.5, 21.5, 21.5)
(23.5, 25.5, 25.5, 26.5) cm
12¾ (13, 13, 13¼)
(13¼, 13¼, 13½, 13½)"
32.5 (33, 33, 33.5)
(33.5, 33.5, 34.5, 34.5) cm
SLEEVE
from yoke
12 (12½, 12½, 12½) (13¾, 14¾, 14¾, 15½)"
30.5 (32, 32, 32) (35, 37.5, 37.5, 39.5) cm

***Note:** Pieces are worked from the top down.*

Divide for Body and Sleeves

Dividing Rnd: K36 (40, 43, 47) (51, 54, 58, 60), place next 42 (44, 44, 44) (48, 52, 52, 54) sts on holder or waste yarn for left sleeve, k73 (81, 86, 94) (102, 109, 116, 121) sts for front, place next 42 (44, 44, 44) (48, 52, 52, 54) sts on holder or waste yarn for right sleeve, k37 (41, 43, 47) (51, 55, 58, 61) sts for second half of back—146 (162, 172, 188) (204, 218, 232, 242) sts remain.

BODY

Work even until piece measures 11¾ (11½, 11½, 11½) (11¾, 12, 12½, 12¾)" [30 (29, 29, 29) (30, 30.5, 32, 32.5) cm], or to 5½" [14 cm] less than desired back length from underarm.

Split Hem

Dividing Rnd: K36 (40, 43, 47) (51, 54, 58, 60), k73 (81, 86, 94) (102, 109, 116, 121) sts for front and place front sts on holder or waste yarn, knit to beginning-of-rnd marker, remove marker, knit to end—73 (81, 86, 94) (102, 109, 116, 121) sts remain for back.

BACK

Set-Up Row (WS): P1, M1L 0 (0, 1, 1) (1, 0, 1, 0) time(s), purl to end—73 (81, 87, 95) (103, 109, 117, 121) sts.

Begin Flat Linen Stitch; work even for 5½" (14 cm), ending with a WS row.

BO all sts loosely.

FRONT

With WS facing, transfer front sts to needle. Rejoin yarn ready to work a WS row.

Set-Up Row (WS): P1, M1L 0 (0, 1, 1) (1, 0, 1, 0) time(s), purl to end—73 (81, 87, 95) (103, 109, 117, 121) sts.

Begin Flat Linen Stitch; work even for 3½" (9 cm), ending with a WS row.

BO all sts loosely.

SLEEVES

With RS facing, transfer sleeve sts to needle(s) in your preferred style for working in the rnd. Rejoin yarn at center underarm; pm for beginning of rnd.

Note: It might be helpful to measure your wrist at this point and compare your wrist measurement to the wrist circumference in the schematic. If you would like to give yourself a little more room at the wrist, simply omit the decrease rnd and work in St st to the beginning of the cuff. If you would like even more room at the wrist, consider increasing 2 sts on the last rnd before beginning the cuff.

Knit 1 rnd.

Decrease Rnd: K2, k2tog, knit to last 3 sts, ssk, k1—40 (42, 42, 42) (46, 50, 50, 52) sts remain.

All other rounds: knit all stitches, slipping markers as you come to them.

Work even until piece measures 9¼ (9½, 9½, 9¾) (9¾, 9¾, 10, 10)" [23.5 (24, 24, 25) (25, 25, 25.5, 25.5) cm], or to 3½" (9 cm) less than desired length from underarm.

Cuff

Begin Circular Linen Stitch; work even for 3½" (9 cm).

BO all sts loosely.

FINISHING

This pullover requires very minimal finishing: Soak in warm water until water is cool. Roll piece in towels to press out water, then lay flat to dry, shaping to schematic measurements. If desired, you can make the halo rise by gently steaming piece once it is completely dry.

Candlemaking in Found Vessels

As an apartment dweller, I have become thoroughly addicted to candles. In lieu of having a crackling fire to gather around, I have begun to collect these flickering stand-ins with relish, choosing scents carefully to cater to my mood and express the season: heady florals and spices, the deep, cooling scent of balsam. I adore the way that something so simple can add to the atmosphere of a space and set the tone for the time spent within it.

I've been more intentional this year than ever in choosing which candles I purchase, seeking out those that are poured into vessels that can be reused and repurposed into planters for seedlings or gift plants for friends. Now that the holidays are approaching, I have gotten excited about the prospect of many of these saved vessels becoming new candles through a very simple, basic candlemaking process. Here's my "method" so you can try the same.

MATERIALS

First, you'll need a variety of found or purchased vessels of various depths and structures. It's my experience that traditional column shapes, not shallow bowls, are the best for candlemaking, and so I've begun scouring thrift shops for decorative jars and old candle holders that might work well. Grab a few more than you think you'll need, as this method isn't exact and you might have some extra wax to pour!

Wicks, available either as traditional coated cord-style or as flat planks of wood. Of the two, the cord style is a little more difficult to wrangle, and I prefer working with the flat, wooden kind.

Wax flakes. I bought mine at a big-box craft store, and they are made of soy. You can find traditional beeswax as well, but these are a lot easier for first-time candlemakers. They should come with instructions for melting in the microwave.

Scents. I have collected a variety of essential oils from various sources, including the grocery store, my yoga teacher, and friends who sell them. While a few drops will do it for aromatherapy applications day to day, you'll need *a lot* of essential oil to make a strongly scented candle (part of the reason the best candles are so expensive). Be prepared and don't overspend on the scents—look for a good deal.

Accents. These are optional, but some people like to add a little bit of flair to their candles in the form of dried flowers, lavender buds, dye in the wax, or more. Feel free to experiment and see what you like and what your style is—just remember that whatever you add is likely to come in contact with flame at some point, so make sure the scent of it burning doesn't chase you out of the house!

The first step in the process is to prepare each of your candles for pouring. For traditional wicks, you'll want to affix them to the bottom of the jar with a bit of wax adhesive or a bit of melted wax (allow it to cool before pouring). I did find it possible for the wooden wicks to stand up on their own, but you'll want to brace them with your hand while pouring to keep them from drifting to one side or the other of the candle. Above all, make sure your wick is fairly secure and stable in the center of your vessel.

You can trim your wicks at this stage if you feel that they're very stable: Trim them about ½" (1.3 cm) above the top of the vessel, and you can retrim closer before the first burn. A sturdy pair of scissors should have no trouble cutting through the wooden wicks.

Next, follow the directions on your soy flake package to microwave the amount of wax needed for your candles. While there are instructions to measure, I have a tendency to just wing it and pour in about 3 cups (385 g) soy flakes, then melt them, stirring as instructed on the wax packaging. You'll have lumps in between stirring and heating sessions, and you want to get them all out before you pour your candles.

It is at this stage that you'll also add fragrance. While most essential oil manufacturers will claim that 1 to 2 drops is enough to infuse scents, I find that a larger concentration is really necessary to make the wax scented: 10 to 20 drops. If you're on a budget or afraid to use essential oils to infuse scent, you can also buy pre-prepared, thinner scents from the same place you buy your wax. Some of my favorite scents are sandalwood, jasmine, lavender, patchouli, and rosemary.

Pour the wax and scent mixture into your candle slowly, taking care not to pour quickly and accidentally shift your wick. If you like, you can pour candles in layers, allowing each candle to cool between the layers and changing the scent from start to finish. This is also a fun place to add dried flowers to your candle so they can be revealed as the candle burns!

Allow the candles to cool, then trim the wicks closer to the surface. You should let your candles "cure" for a while before burning them, and keep them in a cool, dry place until use. Tie a bow on them and give them away as holiday gifts!

fibers for warmth

ALPACA

There are two types of alpaca: Huacaya alpaca is the most common, with fluffy, short fibers that create silky, slinky yarns when used solo, but add a bit of drape and a lot of warmth to any blend. Suri alpaca has a longer staple fiber that blends beautifully with longwools to create shiny, softly haloed yarns. Of the two, Huacaya is easier to find and a little bit warmer, as it is blended into carded, not combed, yarns, which are designed structurally to capture warmth.

ANGORA

The fiber these fluffy bunnies produce is soft and delicate, and when blended with Merino wool, positively decadent. With a high halo and next-to-skin gentleness, a little Angora content can go a long way toward creating a warm, light layer. One hundred percent Angora yarns are probably a little too delicate for a full garment, so I prefer 30 percent Angora or less in most blends.

BISON

Sometimes mislabeled as "buffalo," bison fiber comes from the heavy-headed herd animals of the American plains. This rich, chocolate-colored fiber is exceedingly warm, unusual, and expensive. I love it blended with silk and wool into a fingering weight; those who brave the deepest snows of winter and live in colder climates may discover plenty of room for it in their closets.

CAMEL

Fiber from this desert dromedary has made its way into many beautiful blends and is more readily available than ever before. Fawn in color, camel yarns add depth to dyed yarns and a bit of heathering when blended with wool. Camel and silk is an ultraluxurious pairing that has amazing drape and warmth.

CASHMERE

While not the warmest fiber on this list, cashmere is warmer than wool and is often blended into yarns that retain warmth, thanks to the short staple length of this delicate fiber. A true treat for any crafter, cashmere-blend yarns (or even 100 percent cashmere) are the ultimate in softness.

MOHAIR

The glowing strands of a mohair or mohair-blend yarn are unmistakable, and this fiber (which comes from a goat) has made massive strides in popularity over the past few years as a strand-along yarn, especially when blended with silk. It has the ability to lend radiant color or nuance, as well as warmth, to any project.

QIVIUT

The warmest and most decadent fiber on this list, qiviut is the soft, downy undercoat of the musk ox. Fibers are not shorn but plucked or gathered from the animal, or objects and plants the animal has rubbed up against. This fiber, most commonly found in Canada and Alaska, is often available only as a lace weight, thanks to the delicacy, scarcity, and hefty price tag. While I have felt qiviut, I have not knit with it, so I can't tell you if you're missing out. I imagine it's exceptionally lovely as mitten linings.

YAK

Available in true, deep browns and blended with silk, wool, or even nylon for socks, yak is available in silky, slinky yarn form, or, by using the first shearing of a yak, in delicate, ultrasoft baby yak down. Down is especially warm, and a little can go a long way toward increasing the coziness of any yarn. Remember that this fiber is slightly heavier and denser when spun.

CREATING NEW KNITTERS

I DON'T ENJOY KNITTING FOR other people unless I really like them a lot, there isn't a strict deadline involved, and I get to choose the yarn. While I know many knitters who generously give of their knitting time and actually enjoy making things for people they know, or people they may not know at all, I am simply not one of them. I would much prefer to make something other than a pattern pre-chosen and dictated to me: I would rather make a Knitter.

A Knitter with a capital K is something quite different from a knitter. Lowercase knitters are people who enjoy the way that knitting fits into their lives. These knitters make beautiful things: classic accessories like ribbed beanies and seed-stitch cowls; large-gauge afghans that tumble effortlessly from baskets in the living room; stacks of Stockinette sweaters in a variety of textures and fits that slide seamlessly into any wardrobe. These knitters have the skills to execute everything they want, but they treat their knitting like any other hobby, and reserve it for certain months of the year when they can have the complete seasonal picture: warm beverage in hand, a cat on the lap, and a roaring fire. They see knitting as an experience, and enjoy every moment of it. I love these knitters, and relish their seasonal making each year, their choices of yarns (which they've been collecting all year long), and the careful way they block out their knitting time. They are handmade-couture fashionistas; their vision is clear and they are tailor-making to fit.

A Knitter sees knitting as a lifestyle. This crafter has fallen down the rabbit hole and is delighted to be lost inside the warren. There is too much to explore, and too many things to experience, to adhere strictly to any particular aesthetic. Intarsia, entrelac, stranded knitting, two-at-a-time, Magic Loop, steeking, brioche: The words are an enchantment, each one a task that yields new possibilities and excitements. The Knitter begins with the same steps as all other knitters, but quickly pushes beyond the boundaries of her knowledge and grasps at whichever new thread excites her. Some projects might be flops, but each failure is an opportunity to learn more about the technique, more about the yarn, more about the fiber.

As Knitters begin digging into everything yarn-related, they often pick up a few more fiber hobbies along the way. Some will turn to spinning, to learn how a yarn's structure affects the finished piece, and will get to know the wool more deeply than before. If they continue down this path, they often find themselves playing with color through handspun yarns, or trying a variety of fibers and techniques. Perhaps they'll buy a fleece at market one year and prep it at home, or begin spindle-spinning the finest yarns for frothy, delicate lace.

Other Knitters begin picking up related techniques for fun. They might also become expert crocheters, learn how tatting works, or dig into Tunisian crochet.

They might buy a knitting sheath and belt and see how fast they can go, or swap their technique for making basic stitches for that of another country. They adapt knitting to themselves over time and are clever inventors of new stitches and techniques that will change and expand ideas of what knitting can do. They play with color in unexpected ways, put together intricate, carefully structured designs, and create unbelievable fabrics.

Some Knitters become masters of wardrobe. While many knitters have learned to follow patterns or write their own, Knitters who love the fashion side of the craft will lock on to yarn brands and dye styles, blends, and the way a knitted fabric hangs. They learn the ins and outs of garment construction and altering pieces for fit, choosing just the right final combination of materials to get a high-quality look out of every knit, and enjoy every moment of planning ahead for all the things they can't wait to make. This Knitter can never be restricted by time: There are too many things to do to consign knitting to a single season. They are also the most likely to see yarn as fabric in other ways, and venture into weaving, embroidery, quilting, and sewing as adjacent hobbies.

I taught many, many knitters over the years that my mother and I owned a shop in Iowa, and what I discovered is that those who become Knitters have a few things in common. Often, their lives are undergoing a period of great change when they first learn the skill or pick it up again. Some have moved to a new place. They have relocated far from friends, and sometimes family, and are looking for ways to meet people. Knitting has the added bonus of being a diversion in times of loneliness. It appeals not only to those settling into new places but to those settling into new lives after a bereavement or change in health. Many people come to knitting in a time of need: need for friendship, company, and comfort.

Other Knitters are born out of excitement. They have seen a friend or someone they admire on social media making beautiful things, and they realize with delight that they can create something, too. The craft's last big boom was in 2006, when crafting blogs encouraged knitters to try new skills and new patterns, and Ravelry opened up the internet to yarn crafters in new ways. Now, we're seeing a similar buzz around beautiful Instagram posts that bring knitting to the forefront of style and cozy fun. Knitters who begin in this way find excitement in possibility: Knitting is a creative outlet and becomes a form of self-expression.

Knitters also rise from families of Knitters—families that didn't look at knitting as simply a hobby but passed it down as a skill considered as useful as sewing or baking. Knitters with a family history have a deep well of fond memories to draw on that frame their knitting experience and set the standard for their own moves forward. Knitting has become a part of their internal culture, and has created a way for them to connect themselves with past and future generations. It is these Knitters who have kept the craft alive even through periods of fading popularity: I strive to be one of these, creating both new knitters and new Knitters along the way.

Stranded Knitting Basics

I know there is a "right way" to do many knitting things, and I also know that stranded knitting, a time-established tradition of playing with color in knitting, has a traditional way to make the stitches, manage the strands, and get the right results. There are things to keep in mind, of course, like color dominance: how the yarn is carried along or which yarn is in "front" establishes a sense of precedence for that color in a knitted piece. There are rules about how many stitches can form a float, or about which patterns may be used, to distinguish between various colorwork styles. I'm going to ask those of you reading this book who feel very strongly about these things to skip this section, for your health, but also for mine—I am simply not going to be "doing it right," but rather, doing it the way it works for me, in the hopes that it might work for someone else.

You see, traditional stranded knitting is designed to work well for knitters who have established themselves as able to hold the yarn with the left hand. I am not one of these knitters, or rather, while I can do it, I generally prefer not to. I learned to knit "English," a technique also called throwing, where you toss the yarn around the needle with your right hand and fingers. It works just fine for most things. It's very common, and comfortable, and how a lot of knitters first learn. It has a reputation for being slow, but many "throwers" can also become quite adept at it. Other knitters will find themselves transitioning to Continental knitting, a knitting technique that involves some fiddliness with the left hand but is also speedier and sets you up wonderfully to perform feats of knitting prowess like proper stranded knitting.

Proper stranded knitting technique is to hold two colors at once, one in each hand, tensioned just right, and to work between them as if you

somehow have four hands instead of two. I have attempted it, and while I agree that it is theoretically possible, I prefer instead to stick with what I know; as a result, I present to you my method for stranded knitting as a thrower. Your tension, acceptance, and use of this technique is entirely up in the air, and I understand that, but perhaps it will work for one of the readers of this book, and they will be able to create new and exciting knits, and that is enough for me to include it.

I've set up a little cuff with only two-color ribbing that goes round and round for this illustration—I'm not sure it will ever become anything, but it's perfect for this. Essentially, the first color will be white, and the second color will be blue, but they will be referred to as Color A and Color B, so you can replace them however you like while practicing. Begin by knitting a single stitch in Color A (white), then drop the yarn from your hand and knit the second stitch with Color B (blue).

When you pick up Color A again to work the next stitch, don't worry about the first stitch's tension. You can adjust it from the tail end, or make tiny tension modifications here to make sure everything is nice and snug without being too tight or too loose.

Continue working with Color B for the fourth stitch, and use the same intuition you already have (and you do have it, I promise) to make sure the tension is just right here, too. Continue on in the round, alternating A and B to make the corrugated, two-color rib.

Remember that stranded knitting or color-work knitting is always a bit tighter than the same stitch in a single color, so when you measure gauge remember that it will not stretch or have any ease in the final fabric.

stranded knitting yarns

Stranded knitting gives us endless opportunities to play with color through a variety of shapes and applications. Whether you're eyeing this technique for a traditional Fair Isle sweater, for a pair of Latvian mittens, or for a design of your own creation, the yarn you choose has a considerable bearing on the success of your final piece.

JAMIESON'S OF SHETLAND SPINDRIFT

The exquisite palette of forty-eight colors available in quarter-size skeins makes purchasing (and receiving) any amount of Jamieson's for a colorwork project a bit like getting a box of candies in the mail. From bright poppy red to softly heathered natural black, there is a hue for every project. Jamieson's has been making beautiful yarns for weavers and knitters since 1893, and has been producing a 100 percent Shetland wool product, in Shetland, since the early 1980s. This is a local wool from far away, and I love the sense of history that this yarn exudes. It's not ultrasoft, but certainly softens up with wear.

HARRISVILLE DESIGNS SHETLAND

For the past century, Harrisville Designs in Harrisville, New Hampshire, has been operating one of the United States' few surviving woolen mills, producing a variety of yarns for weaving and knitting, and also building looms. Their yarn Shetland and the worsted-weight counterpart, Highland, are available in a palette of sixty-four exceptional colors perfect for stranded knitting. Spun woolen with a blend of wool breeds (not Shetland) from New Zealand and Australia, this yarn is lofty and light, and gets a better hand with every wash.

ELEMENTAL AFFECTS SHETLAND

If you're looking for the true feel of 100 percent American Shetland, look no further than Jeane deCoster's brand Elemental Affects. Jeane has been working to restore and support individual breed-focused yarns in the United States, and her offerings are always exquisite. Her lineup of Shetland wools is available in full-size 1.8-ounce (50-g) put-ups, or in miniskeins for little accents or crewel embroidery work. Not only is this yarn delightfully affordable, the colors are different from those offered by many other producers. I especially love that the natural Shetland colors (of which there are officially eleven variations) are offered with traditional names like Emsket, Moorit, and Mooskit.

RAUMA FINULLGARN

I would be remiss if I didn't mention a yarn related to my own Norwegian ancestry. Scandinavian countries have a very rich history of colorwork textiles, and each region or country has a unique set of styles and patterns. Finullgarn offers a "traditional Norwegian knitting yarn" in, unbelievably, more than one hundred colors.

Less traditional yarns are just fine for stranded knitting, of course, provided that they have an excellent color range and that the fibers can grab together to create the signature cohesive, smooth fabric and help each motif pop.

ANGORAGARNET

From the early 1940s to the late 1960s, enterprising Emma Jacobsson ran the Bohus Stickning design house to offer work to women in her community in the depressed Bohuslän province of Sweden, over which her husband presided as governor. During that two-decade span, this design house created an exceptional form of stranded knitting that features both knit and purl pattern motifs, realized in Angora-blend yarns, that has become known as Bohus. The soft halo of the Angora, dyed in a range of beautifully coordinated colorways, produced stranded textiles that have a unique, almost watercolor-like

appearance. The complexity and beauty of the original pieces from the design house has encouraged knitters to try their hands at reproducing original Bohus designs as well as to create new Bohus-inspired motifs. Bohuslän-based AngoraGarnet provides modern interpretations of the design house's original colors and also sells kits and individual skeins of its lofty, cruelty-free 50 percent Merino, 50 percent Angora blend in around one hundred colors.

RETROSARIA MONDIM

This heritage breed–focused Portuguese knitting company has taken the yarn world by storm with a variety of unusual and beautiful wool and wool-blend yarns. One of my current favorites, Mondim, is an ideal stranded-knitting yarn for folks who can't tolerate any scratchiness or halo. Spun using 100 percent Fine Portuguese Wool, this yarn has an almost cottony feel, but still maintains a bit of tooth for grabbing onto nearby colors. With a small palette of thirty colors, both solid and speckled, this yarn offers new opportunities for a modern take on traditional motifs.

BROOKLYN TWEED PEERIE

While I generally steer clear of smooth yarns for colorwork, Brooklyn Tweed's all-American Peerie, spun with soft Merino, is irresistibly suited to stranded motifs. The Merino used still maintains a bit of its wooliness, allowing it to stick to nearby colors and create cohesive fabrics while remaining next-to-skin soft. I love the carefully curated palette (forty-five colors to choose from) and the finished, smooth appearance of the fabric knit at tight gauges. Loft is another delightful Brooklyn Tweed yarn suitable for colorwork, for those seeking a more heathery look.

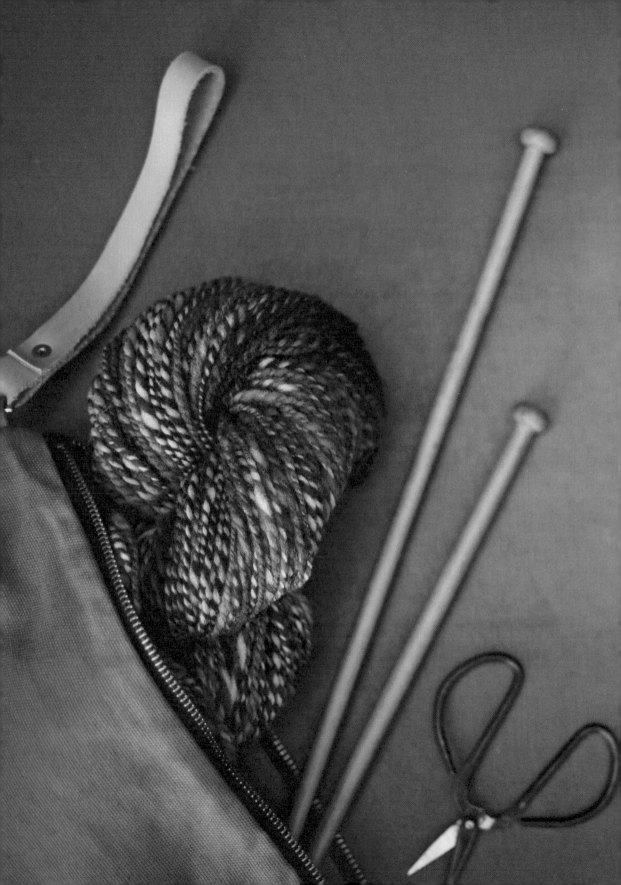

a beginning knitter's kit

APPROACHABLE YARN

For knitters just starting out, look for yarns that have a high wool content, and nothing "tricky" like too much silk or a heavily haloed fiber. Wool has higher elasticity than most fibers, making it easier to manipulate when stitches are a bit too tight. Haloed yarns tend to grip each other, creating a more secure fabric that is harder to unravel—a task your beginner will likely do at least a few times. In contrast, silky or slinky yarns will move too quickly on the needle and increase the risk of dropped stitches. Some of my favorite beginner wool breeds are Merino, for the knitter who loves softness; Corriedale, for those looking to experience the farm a little more closely; and Targhee, for those who delight in bouncy stitches.

I feel that DK- and worsted-weight yarns are always the easiest to learn on. If you go too big with a chunky or bulky yarn, the small variations in beginners' stitches will seem like massive, glaring errors: A single dropped stitch in a worsted-weight scarf can disappear, while the same mistake in bulky fabrics leaves a large hole. Small yarns have the opposite effect, hiding the knitter's stitches so well that they are difficult for beginners to find. When you're learning to read your knitting, it helps to have a nice, medium-size "text" to study!

COMFORTABLE NEEDLES

While we all develop our own preferences for needle material, it's easy to choose needles for those just starting out. For beginners, I prefer a needle with a bit of give and a medium point. I've been able to find the perfect match in bamboo and wooden needles. While aluminum and acrylic needles are easy to come by and inexpensive, they are usually too slick for knitters who might begin with extremely tight or loose tension.

It's fairly traditional to get new knitters started with straight needles, and I see no major reason to break with tradition here, either. However, if you find that your knitter is prone to slipping stitches off the end and forgetting them, you might consider switching to a shorter (24" [61 cm]) circular needle and giving her a set of needle stoppers as well.

A BRIGHT-COLORED STITCH MARKER

Beginners have a very hard time knowing which side of the fabric they're on, and a common mistake is turning mid-row and heading back the other way. Help them along by giving them a pretty or bright-colored stitch marker to help identify which side is which. A locking stitch marker is best here—I've had a few beginners knit their closed-ring markers into their projects.

A PRETTY PROJECT BAG

Give them somewhere to store their knitting safely and pull together your package at the same time with a pretty project bag. Drawstring or zipper-top bags are especially nice for beginners since they tend to keep everything contained, but if you've started them off with long straight needles, you may want to go with an open-top bucket or tote style.

AN EASY PATTERN

There will be time later to teach your new knitter about gauge, changing color, and doing fancy stitches. An easy pattern that features only knit and purl stitches is best for starting out. While most knitters' first projects are scarves or dishcloths, I'm a fan of single-loop cowls that are seamed when they reach the ideal length. These projects are a try-on-as-you-go option and are just long enough to get some practice in before beginners get bored.

Maple Sugar Cowl

/ About the Yarn /

BARRETT WOOL CO. HOME: FINGERING WEIGHT

Springy, spongy, and appealing, Barrett Wool Co.'s flagship base, Home, is perfect for knitters who love familiarizing themselves with a single wool that can serve a variety of purposes. This yarn is produced entirely within the United States and comes in two transmutable weights: The fingering could easily stand in for sport thanks to a bit of bounciness, and the worsted could easily pass as an especially exuberant DK weight. This makes Home a great choice for a variety of projects, from socks, shawls, and sweaters to the adorable toy knits that cofounder Susan B. Anderson designs.

Barrett Wool Co. is headquartered in Wisconsin, where Susan and her son are able to work side by side to bring her colorful vision to life. Home comes in a palette of shades that swing easily into any project: a pink just pale enough to be sophisticated for a simple sweater, or delicate for a feminine baby gift; the perfect shade of flannel red for a classic hat, or the dapper sweater of a stuffed moose. Susan has put her decades-long tenure as a designer in the industry to use with this beautifully designed brand.

I wanted to feel the delightful bounce of this yarn right against my skin; it's the Goldilocks level of woolliness; not the least bit scratchy, but far from slinky or superwashed. This is 100 percent wool, no doubt about it, and it shows in every stitch on this textured, cozy cowl. I've used a favorite stitch with a boring name: the Diagonal Crossed Stitch, which in this color reminds me a bit of brown sugar (or maple sugar) candies.

SIZES
One size

FINISHED MEASUREMENTS
16¾" (42.5 cm) circumference at top edge; × 21" (53 cm) at longest point, not including tassels

YARN
Barrett Wool Co. Home Fingering Weight [100% American wool; 370 yards (338 meters)/3.5 ounces (100 grams)]: 2 skeins Bear

ALTERNATIVE YARNS
515 yards (471 meters) in a fingering-weight yarn, including tassels

(AU) Millpost Merino (100% superfine Merino wool, permaculture-grown)

(Peru) Pichinku Fibers Qanchis Skinny (80% Merino wool, 20% baby alpaca)

(USA) Brooklyn Tweed Peerie (100% USA-grown Merino wool)

Look for something round and bouncy that will show off every stitch, and don't be afraid to dig through your stash and try something unexpected. Handspun with a nubbled texture or a slinky alpaca or silk blend will add different dimensions to this cowl's versatile shape and stitches.

NEEDLES
Size US 6 (4 mm) circular needle, 16" (40 cm) long

Change needle size if necessary to obtain correct gauge.

NOTIONS

2 stitch markers

GAUGE

24 sts and 36 rows = 4" (10 cm) in Flat Diagonal Crossed Stitch, blocked

PATTERN NOTES

This cowl is worked in the round from the top down, and then one side is narrowed to a point with the use of short rows. Tassels are added to weigh down the point and give a finished touch and lend to the bandana look.

The short rows used to shape the front of the cowl may feel different than other short rows you have tried. They have been modified to work more effectively within this pattern. They do not require wraps, which helps them to hide in the fabric. Resolving the short rows will require you to read your knitting and understand the Diagonal Crossed Stitch pattern so that you can stay in pattern as you resolve each short row. Pay attention to what step in the pattern you have completed before you work the Resolution Round.

SPECIAL ABBREVIATIONS

WC (work cross): Slip 1, k1, yo, pass slipped st over both k1 and yo.

STITCH PATTERNS

GARTER RIB

(multiple of 5 sts; 2-rnd repeat)
Rnd 1: Knit.
Rnd 2: *K1, p4; repeat from * to last 4 sts, p4.
Repeat Rnds 1 and 2 for Garter Stitch Rib.

CIRCULAR DIAGONAL CROSSED STITCH

(even number of sts; 4-rnd repeat)
Rnd 1: *WC; repeat from * to end.
Rnd 2: Knit.
Rnd 3: K1, *WC; repeat from * to last st, k1.
Rnd 4: Knit.
Repeat Rnds 1–4 for Circular Diagonal Crossed Stitch.

FLAT DIAGONAL CROSSED STITCH

(even number of sts; 4-row repeat)
Row 1 (RS): *WC; repeat from * to end.
Row 2: Purl.
Row 3: K1, *WC; repeat from * to last st, k1.
Row 4: Purl.
Repeat Rows 1–4 for Flat Diagonal Crossed Stitch.

COWL

Using a semi-stretchy CO, CO 100 sts. Join for working in the rnd, being careful not to twist sts; pm for beginning of rnd (marker is at center back).

Begin Garter Rib; work even for 7 rnds.

Change to Circular Diagonal Crossed Stitch; work even until piece measures approximately 7½" (19 cm) from the beginning, ending with Rnd 2 of pattern.

Shape Cowl

Note: *Change to Flat Diagonal Crossed Stitch, beginning with row following last rnd worked.*

Short-Row 1 (RS): Work 26 sts in pattern, pm, work 48 sts in pattern, pm, turn.

Short-Row 2 (WS): Purl to 2 sts before marker, turn.

Short-Row 3: Slip 2 sts purlwise wyib, k1, *WC; repeat from * to 3 sts before gap, k1, turn.

Short-Row 4: Slip 2 sts purlwise wyif, purl to 2 sts before gap, turn.

Short-Row 5: Slip 2 sts purlwise wyib, *WC; repeat from * to 2 sts before gap, turn.

Short-Row 6: Slip 2 sts purlwise wyif, purl to 2 sts before gap, turn.

Repeat Short-Rows 5 and 6 four more times; 8 sts remain between gaps.

Resolution Rnd: K1, *[WC] 26 times [3 times across sts between gaps, 11 times to resolve gaps from short rows (removing marker while resolving last gap), and 12 times to beginning-of-rnd marker.

Next Rnd: Knit, resolving remaining gaps as you come to them.

Change to Garter Stitch Rib; work even for 1" (2.5 cm).

BO all sts.

FINISHING

Block piece as desired.

Tassels (optional)

Wind yarn approximately 226 times (or to desired thickness) around a piece of cardboard 4" (10 cm) long. Slide a single strand of yarn under the strands at the top of the tassel; tie tightly, leaving ends long enough for attaching Tassel to Cowl. Cut through all strands at the bottom end. Tie a second piece of yarn tightly around the Tassel several times, approximately ½" (1.3 cm) from top of Tassel; secure ends inside top of Tassel. Attach to Cowl and trim ends even.

COZY MAKING RITUALS

I AM A FIRM BELIEVER that we should feel the season we're in, even when we're indoors. In May, when the first hot day comes and every store, movie theater, and shop puts the air-conditioning on full-blast, I grumble about fresh air. As soon as the summer heat breaks and delivers chilly autumn evenings, I get out all the quilts and blankets and leave the windows open all night long. When winter finally arrives, I leave the heat low and relish cozy making rituals.

Knitting is a culture in and of itself, and we have our own traditions and rituals that welcome the deepest, darkest parts of winter with delight and wonder. Having brought out our handknits at the first fall chill, we're ready to begin wearing the heavier ones by mid-December. As our thoughts turn toward the time of year we'll spend the most hours with family and friends in tight spaces, we also seek the comfort of familiarity in our clothing. Favorite sweaters, like favorite boots, fit just the right way. You know their texture intimately, having spent hundreds of hours handling and molding them into final form. A hat, scarf, or cowl is a friend you bring home from college to meet the family. A sweater is a long-term relationship.

Welcoming sweaters back into your rotation is a cherished moment. I love digging these garments out of storage and bringing them into the light again, each stitch to be celebrated. My memories are wound around every purl, and twisted into every cable cross. Pulling out each sweater is the same as thumbing through the family album, the faces familiar but happier, fresher versions of themselves. We don't love them any less for the experiences they've been through and shared with us.

Settling back into the habits of the season means practicing some of our coziest making rituals. Rising from a bed laden with blankets, sliding stockinged toes into house slippers, and making a pot of coffee are some of my favorites. I love to take it all in from the dining room table, my hands wrapped around a hot mug and my fingertips peering out from sweater cuffs. I watch as the cat crouches and chitters at birds feasting on sunflower seeds on the other side of the glass door. I absorb the glitter of frost around the edge of the windows and on the grass. These quiet moments help me prepare for the day in a season that beckons me to sleep in, to curl up under a big blanket on the couch and knit and watch silly holiday movies.

During the first few months of winter, I try to pull all the afghans and blankets out of rotation and put them through a good wash, either at home or at the local laundromat. While sheets and pillowcases get washed frequently, these upper layers are often ignored or smell a bit musty after coming out of storage. Lavender-infused laundry soap is a key element to my happiness here: There is nothing quite like curling up under a big blanket that provides comfort both physically and through the magic of aromatherapy. If you use woolen dryer balls, you can add a few drops of your favorite essential oils to these as a replacement for scented dryer sheets!

I try to complete chores and tasks in the mornings so that my evenings, which come sooner with the change in seasons, are free for relaxing. Although it takes some gumption to get out the door in frigid temperatures, this makes the return to our own warm nests all the sweeter. I maximize my time to knit in the evenings by preparing foods that are easily left alone: a roasted chicken and root veggies need to be checked on only twice; a slow cooker of stew or soup makes the most of an afternoon alone. Add in some crusty bread and settle into seasonal food. It is always winter when I think about the benefits of kitchen gardening and canning, and hope to do more the next year. Perhaps I should start planning my gardens in mid-January so I don't forget come spring.

Above all, winter is about timing. While the rest of the year is busy and full, I try to keep this season free of travel other than for the holidays, preferring to tuck in at home and focus on indoor projects. This is the perfect time of year to rethink your storage options or reorganize. It's ideal for pulling out languishing projects and getting them up to speed, or casting on something new. Think of the season as a call to do more slow making and less planning. Embrace this moment to sit still, stay warm, and rejuvenate.

Sinnet Mitts

/ About the Yarn /

RETROSARIA (ROSA POMAR): BRUSCA

I love any opportunity to try a breed-specific yarn from another country, especially a country that I have so often dreamed of visiting. Portugal seems to be such a culturally rich and artistic place from far away, and Rosa Pomar absolutely captures the bohemian aesthetic often associated with her home through her beautifully hand-illustrated yarn labeling and thoughtfully selected colors. What makes this yarn so special, though, is that each skein helps promote the rejuvenation and preservation of wool production in Portugal for more than just rugs and tapestries.

Brusca is a breed-specific wool that focuses on a sheep: the Saloia, which is native to Lisbon and Setúbal. This Mediterranean sheep is actually in decline, and it excites me that by purchasing this yarn, in some way we can help promote the preservation of this breed, which is a multipurpose animal also known for dairy production. Saloia has Merino blood in its heritage, and it's no surprise that the fiber blends beautifully with the naturally colored Merino that makes up the other half of the yarn. Potentially a mix of pure white Merino and maybe some pale grays and darker grays, the resulting yarn has an incredibly soft hand that might surprise those who have only seen and not touched it—spun as a 2-ply with a bit of rusticity, Brusca has character that shows in every stitch.

SIZES

Small (Medium, Large, X-Large)

FINISHED MEASUREMENTS

7½ (8¼, 9¼, 10)" [19 (21, 23.5, 25.5) cm] hand circumference

YARN

Retrosaria Brusca [50% Saloia/ 50% Merino wool); 136 yards (125 meters)/1.8 ounces (50 grams)]: 1 (2, 2, 2) skein(s) #13A

ALTERNATIVE YARNS

140 (155, 170, 185) yards [128 (142, 155, 169) meters in a DK-weight yarn

If replacing with another yarn, I'd recommend farm yarns that are rustic but soft to achieve a similar look, or a nice woolen handspun 2-ply. If you would like crisper stitches, change to a yarn that has more plies but the same gauge to get a totally different and very elegant looking mitt. Luxury blends would be fantastic here, too!

(FR) Biches et Bûches Le Cashmere & Lambswool (87.5% lambswool, 12.5% cashmere)

(USA) A Verb for Keeping Warm Flock (100% California wool)

(USA) Woolfolk Tynd (100% Merino wool)

NEEDLES

Size US 5 (3.75 mm) needle(s) in your preferred style for working in the rnd

Change needle size if necessary to obtain correct gauge.

NOTIONS

Stitch markers; stitch holder or waste yarn

GAUGE

24 sts and 32 rnds = 4" (10 cm) in Mixed Rib Stitch, washed and dried flat

PATTERN NOTES

If you prefer to work in the round using double-pointed needles, you might wish to work the cast-on and first row on a circular needle to make it easier to work with the large number of stitches. If you're having trouble with the twisted stitches, use a needle(s) with a sharper point.

There is no real need to block these mitts before wearing, as your hands will do enough stretching and blocking on their own; but if you want to gift them, soak in warm water to give the wool a little bloom, then lay flat to dry.

SPECIAL TECHNIQUES

To cast on a purl stitch: Insert the tip of the right-hand needle from back to front under the back strand of yarn coming from the forefinger, hook the back strand of yarn coming from the thumb from front to back, and draw it through the loop on your forefinger; remove your forefinger from the loop and pull on the working yarn to tighten the new stitch on the right-hand needle; return your thumb and forefinger to their original positions.

To cast on a knit stitch: Insert the tip of the right-hand needle under the front strand of yarn coming from the thumb from front to back, hook the front strand of yarn coming from the forefinger from back to front, and draw it through the loop on your thumb; remove your thumb from the loop and pull on the working yarn to tighten the new stitch on the right-hand needle; return your thumb and forefinger to their original positions.

STITCH PATTERN
MIXED RIB
(multiple of 5 sts; 2-rnd repeat)
Rnd 1: *K2, p1, k1-tbl, p1; repeat from * to end.
Rnd 2: *Slip 2, p1, k1-tbl, p1; repeat from * to end.
Repeat Rnds 1 and 2 for Mixed Rib.

MITT

Wrist

Note: *Use your preferred method of working in the rnd.*

Using Alternating Long-Tail CO or a stretchy CO of your choice, CO 44 (50, 56, 62) sts as follows: *CO 1 knit st (slipknot counts as first knit st), CO 1 purl st; repeat from * to end. Do not join.

Set-Up Row (WS): *K1, p1-tbl; repeat from * to end.

With RS facing, join for working in the rnd, being careful not to twist sts; pm for beginning of rnd.

Next Rnd: *K1-tbl, p1; repeat from * to end.

Work even until piece measures 1 (1, 1½, 1½)" [2.5 (2.5, 4, 4) cm] from the beginning.

Knit 1 rnd, increasing 1 (0, 0, 0) st(s) or decreasing 0 (0, 2, 2) sts evenly spaced—45 (50, 55, 60) sts.

Change to Mixed Rib; work even until piece measures 8½" (21.5 cm), or to 5" (12.5 cm) from inner elbow, ending with Rnd 2.

SHAPE THUMB GUSSET

Rnd 1: K2, pm, M1P, p1, k1-tbl, p1, M1P, pm, k2, work as established to end—47 (52, 57, 62) sts.

Rnd 2: Slip 2, sm, p2, k1-tbl, p2, sm, work as established to end.

Rnd 3: K2, sm, M1P, purl to twisted st, k1-tbl, purl to marker, M1P, sm, k2, work to end—2 sts increased.

Rnd 4: Slip 2, sm, purl to twisted st, k1-tbl, purl to marker, sm, slip 2, work to end.

Repeat Rnds 3 and 4 two (2, 3, 3) more times—53 (58, 65, 70) sts; 11 (11, 13, 13) sts for thumb gusset.

HAND

Next Rnd: K2, remove marker, place next 11 (11, 13, 13) sts on st holder or waste yarn for thumb, CO 3 sts over gap using Backwards Loop CO, work to end—45 (50, 55, 60) sts remain.

Work even until piece measures approximately 10" (25.5 cm) from the beginning, or to ½" (1.3 cm) less than desired finished length.

Set-Up Rnd: *P1, k1-tbl; repeat from * to last 3 (0, 3, 0) sts, [p1, k2tog-tbl] 1 (0, 1, 0) time(s)—44 (50, 54, 60) sts.

Sizes Small and Medium Only

Next Rnd: *P1, k1-tbl; repeat from * to end.

Sizes Large and X-Large Only

Next Rnd: *K1-tbl, p1; repeat from * to end.

All Sizes

Work even for ½" (1.3 cm).

BO all sts in pattern.

THUMB

Transfer sts from st holder to needle(s). Rejoin yarn at gap, pick up and knit 3 sts from sts CO over gap, pm for beg of rnd—14 (14, 16, 16) sts.

Next Rnd: *P1, k1-tbl; repeat from * to end.

Work even for ½" (1.3 cm).

BO all sts in pattern.

FINISHING

No blocking is necessary; these mitts will block out with wear.

a season of gifting

November ushers in an often-unwelcome sense of imbalance and hurriedness. All year long, I have attempted to be grounded, measured, and careful. I have spent wisely and invested in items that bring me uncluttered happiness. Then, suddenly, the holiday season begins, whirling in with its messaging of *must have*, *want*, and *simply cannot live without*. My peaceful, inspirational social media are inundated with advertisements from all directions: a scrolling, endless digital shopping excursion from my living room chair. What we are not buying, we are pressured to make ourselves. Never mind the sweater you have been aching to finish during your holiday work reprieve.

As knitters, we are told that love is wrapped into every stitch of what we are making, and that a handmade gift is a way to bestow that love on others. You wouldn't want your family and friends to get a *store-bought* gift when you could make them something instead, *would you*? So we buy yarn that we didn't already have in stash, and we fill up our time with projects we wouldn't have made otherwise, and we dedicate every personal moment to the development of a gift for someone else. Someone who might not even wear it. I propose a deviation in tradition, friends. I would like to bring the focus of this season back to gifting, but gifting in a different way.

I would like to begin by gifting myself with the permission to actually enjoy the season. I want to spend my time on the things that I receive the most reward from: games that take over the dining room table. Laughter over a near-empty bottle of wine. Family history told fireside while thumbing through old photo albums. I will allow myself to let go of traditions that bring me stress. If they are important to the family, someone else can step in and take them up, and I can relinquish control for a year in favor of my own sanity. I am giving myself the gift of rest, space, and time.

I find that the gifts I most love to receive during the holidays are those that remind me to calm down and practice self-care in the midst of these busy weeks. Candles that set the mood for my home, imparting subtle scents or a simple, warm glow, are always welcome. A new addition to my skin care regimen, decadent bath oils, or a warm hot water bottle in the small of my back at the end of the day become welcome rituals that make me feel loved and appreciated by myself. I encourage those of you who find little time for yourselves to request the gift of personal space this season from your family members.

I find that rest and relaxation become more possible when we are able to relinquish control. Traditions that will fail without your involvement are not traditions at all. If they are important to your relatives, someone else will take up the mantle of cooking, hosting, or arranging—don't be afraid to let go and discover that what has been stressing you out was all along not that important to those around you. If you find yourself missing it, take solace in the knowledge that it can always return next year.

The act of thoughtful, intentional making of things can be the ideal counterpoint to the commercialism that pervades the world around us from November through January. Whether you end up making for yourself, or choose to make something for someone else, keep in mind that you are already giving so much: your time, your patience, your knowledge. Don't devalue any of these gifts in the rush of a world that seeks to make requirements of arbitrary, truly unneeded things, things that beckon us to reach into our pockets when we should instead be reaching outward to those around us.

things to include when you gift knits

I'm going to admit that I am not much of a gift knitter. I'm not sure if it's because I am more selfish with my crafting time and my materials, or if it's simply because I seem to always be a bit behind the curve. Although I rarely gift my finished handmade items to others, I often think about how to best present them when I do, and so I've got a little list of things that you might consider adding on when you give a knitted gift!

WASHING INSTRUCTIONS AND WOOL WASH

Including washing instructions is essential. For superwash items that you know will get thrown in the wash, recommend that they be laundered on the delicate cycle and tumble-dried low, as I have heard of some superwash wools (and especially superwash blends) that felt when treated with unnecessary roughness. For items that should be handwashed, I like to include a tiny bottle or packet of my favorite wool wash to which I tie a tag giving simple washing instructions: Wash in a lukewarm bath, do not agitate, push out extra water gently, and lay flat to dry.

REPAIR YARN

When knitting for a friend who makes things or just appreciates handmade goods, I keep a little bit of extra yarn in my stash for repairs in case something gets snagged or damaged, and simply indicate that the recipient should follow up if the item is in need of attention. However, if you're gifting to someone you don't know or who you know can do the work, a manila tag with a bit of the yarn wrapped around it could be a handy addition to your gift package!

HANDMADE DETAILS AND ADD-ONS

I have fallen quite in love with the idea of adding a leather, wooden, or twill tag to knitted items I'm gifting, simply for the extra finish these items provide. These little tags are easy to pick up online, in shops for handmade goods, and can even be custom laser-engraved or imprinted with your name or message. Popular sentiments include phrases like "handmade" or "knit with love," and I have also seen small icons included.

CONTACT CARD

In the event that the recipient doesn't know you well enough to have your contact information, including a small card or note with your email address or phone number can ensure that items in need of repair (or questions about the care of an item) come back to you.

FADING SNOWS

I CAN'T SAY THAT I'VE ever been sad to see a winter end. As each winter wears on, it somehow becomes more bitter and grating, and the wind colder and harsher. Each day adds a bit of weariness to my bones. I whine a lot about the weather when it's mid-March and I haven't seen sparkling sunshine in months. In Iowa, spring sometimes doesn't show her bleary eyes until mid-May. Living in the Midwest teaches you about real winters, the kind that dwell in the upper part of the Northern Hemisphere.

Real winters start out fluffy and soft, transitioning overnight from autumn splendor to glittering, blinding wonderlands. I had never seen snow anywhere we lived that was more than a few inches deep. Even when I was living in northern Virginia, the deepest snow I experienced was 6" (15 cm). The first snowfall when I was living in Iowa was 3' (90 cm). My sister and I, both high school students, were astounded. The world outside looked just like a cartoon: lavender skies, and everything white and clean as far as the eye could see. Our joy was compounded by the revelation that it was actually possible to push a ball of snow around the yard and make a snowman. (We thought it was one of those things Hollywood might have made up.)

These first beautiful, glimmering days are even more magical if they begin early in the holiday season. Snow for Thanksgiving, snow for Yule, Ramadan, and Christmas. People get their lights up and have their houses decorated early in the fall. (We thought this was a cute, old-town America tradition. It's actually because if you don't get the lights up now, you have to get them up in the snow.) I love seeing how my neighbors commit to their holiday displays—when I was a kid we used to drive around and look at the lights in our suburb.

In small-town Iowa, you could drive through the whole town. One year, a kid in one of Marshalltown's neighborhoods designed a light display synchronized to music he transmitted on an empty low-frequency radio station. It was nuts and made the national news, and other people started doing it all over the country. There would be a line of traffic stretching out of town, with people listening to the same Christmas music loop as they waited to drive by the display. Afterward, you could go home and have hot chocolate next to the fire.

Almost every house I visited in Iowa had a fireplace or a woodstove. In the South, we have fireplaces, but fewer people use them to fully heat their houses in winter, instead opting to turn up the central heat. I am sure that central heating is better for the environment than a woodstove (although crackling wood is so charming and warming), but a lot of people use gas fireplaces, too. Their design has come a long way from the cheesy gas stoves of the 1990s in which the logs would flicker and glow at regular intervals. Now, sleek inset glass allows you to see through both sides of the fireplace, and the flickering among the real-looking gas logs is positively magical.

As the winter wears on, though, things get harder and harder to bear. Each day gets progressively longer and colder, with an occasional teasing break in temperature of a few degrees, then a hard plummet back into chapping winds and icy afternoons. Occasionally a bit of sun will appear and give everyone reason to hope that spring may be just around the corner. These golden rays are a mirage, and shine down cooly on the world—the snow now gray with silt and slush, piles in odd places that have gone glossy, unmoving cement glaciers that take up one-fourth of the parking spaces in every lot. Salt crunches underfoot and there is a constant kicking, shaking, shuffling dance that must be completed in every doorway. The sun that comes isn't warm enough to melt this deep, encrusted winter.

When at last the temperature does rise, midwesterners seem to give in to the idea of spring reluctantly at first, then all at once. If the temperature rises above 50°F (10°C) consistently for more than a week, suddenly everyone is wearing shorts and T-shirts in bright, happy colors, and swapping out snow boots for rain boots. For another month, they will continue to be both delighted and discouraged by mud or rain season, as snow arrives instead of rain, or sometimes as the dreaded "wintry mix" of both together. Eventually, this deluge will give way to actual warmth, and spring will have arrived, grumpy and sleepy, gray at first and then brighter and stronger toward summer.

It can't be a coincidence that so many people from far northern countries immigrate to places whose climates are similar. They have discovered that while there is a bit of misery, there is also joy in a true winter, a real winter: the reminder that every inch of us is alive and exhilarating in survival in an impossible place. There is a wildness to winters in the northern and midwestern United States that makes each day feel like a battle with the elements, and each amount of warmth that can be collected is a winning point. Discomfort is a feeling that can be endured, and must be endured, but ultimately it leads us to cozy spaces, perfectly prepared for our arrival and delight.

Knitting has deep roots in Scandinavia, and Scandinavians carried the love of fiber arts with them as they colonized parts of modern-day America and Canada. My ancestors were somewhere in that mix, and, living near so many families of Norwegian

and German heritage, I felt closer to them than ever. I could finally make sense of the photos I had seen of my grandfather's upbringing in Wisconsin, and of why my great-great-aunt made it through only a few winters in Red Lodge, Montana, before buying a train ticket home. I had a hard time for the nine years that I spent, off and on, in Iowa, but now that I rarely see real winter weather, I miss it.

Something deep in my core fell in love with real winter. I think that part is also the knitter in me. Maybe that feeling is a tether back through my line of ancestors, a family memory of what it's like to get through a hard winter, and a harder winter, and survive. The knitter comes to the challenge with an advantage: the ability to keep others warm. It is this usefulness of the act that has become my passion that makes me dream of moving north and settling in New Hampshire or Maine or Vermont. In the heat of summer, I dream of fading snows.

abbreviations

BO – Bind off

CO – Cast on

K – Knit

K1-tbl – Knit 1 stitch through the back loop.

K2tog – Knit 2 stitches together.

M1L (make 1—left slanting) – With the tip of the left-hand needle inserted from front to back, lift the strand between the 2 needles onto the left-hand needle; knit the strand through the back loop to increase 1 stitch.

M1P (make 1 purlwise) – With the tip of the left-hand needle inserted from back to front, lift the strand between the 2 needles onto the left-hand needle; purl the strand through the front loop to increase 1 stitch.

M1R (make 1—right slanting) – With the tip of the left-hand needle inserted from back to front, lift the strand between the 2 needles onto the left-hand needle; knit the strand through the front loop to increase 1 stitch.

P – Purl

P2tog – Purl 2 stitches together.

P1tbl – Purl 1 stitch through the back loop.

Pm – Place marker

Rnd(s) – Round(s)

RS – Right side

Sm – Slip marker

Ssk (slip, slip, knit) – Slip the next 2 stitches to the right-hand needle one at a time as if to knit; return them to the left-hand needle one at a time in their new orientation; knit them together through the back loops.

Ssp (slip, slip, purl) – Slip the next 2 stitches to the right-hand needle one at a time as if to knit; return them to the left-hand needle one at a time in their new orientation; purl them together through the back loops.

St st – Stockinette stitch

St(s) – Stitch(es)

Tbl – Through the back loop

WS – Wrong side

Wyib – With yarn in back

Wyif – With yarn in front

Yo – Yarnover

special techniques

ALTERNATING LONG-TAIL CO

Leaving a tail with about 1" (2.5 cm) of yarn for each stitch to be cast on, make a slipknot in the yarn and place it on the right-hand needle (this counts as the first knit stitch cast-on), with the tail to the front and the working end to the back. Insert the thumb and forefinger of your left hand between the strands of yarn so that the working end is around your forefinger and the tail end is around your thumb, "slingshot" fashion. You can find a video here: https://www.youtube.com/watch?v=L7MKMlzVNzM.

To cast on a purl stitch: Insert the tip of the right-hand needle from back to front under the back strand of yarn coming from the forefinger, hook the back strand of yarn coming from the thumb from front to back, and draw it through the loop on your forefinger; remove your forefinger from the loop and pull on the working yarn to tighten the new stitch on the right-hand needle; return your thumb and forefinger to their original positions.

To cast on a knit stitch: Insert the tip of the right-hand needle under the front strand of yarn coming from the thumb from front to back, hook the front strand of yarn coming from the forefinger from back to front, and draw it through the loop on your thumb; remove your thumb from the loop and pull on the working yarn to tighten the new stitch on the right-hand needle; return your thumb and forefinger to their original positions.

BACKWARDS LOOP CO

Make a loop (using a slipknot) with the working yarn and place it on the right-hand needle (first stitch cast-on), *wind yarn around thumb clockwise, insert right-hand needle into the front of the loop on thumb, remove thumb and tighten stitch on needle; repeat from * for remaining stitches to be cast on, or for casting on at the end of a row in progress. You can find a video here: https://www.youtube.com/watch?v=dDfrvqQBGbE.

JENY'S SUPER STRETCHY CAST-ON

Jeny Staiman created this cast-on technique as an alternative, ultrastretchy cast-on. It involves creating a series of individual slip-knots on your needle. While tricky at first, this cast-on is invaluable for socks. You can find Jeny's original video for it here: https://youtu.be/3n8E3I6Cg2k.

KITCHENER STITCH

Kitchener stitch is used to graft two live "halves" of a piece together, and it's most often seen when grafting the toes of socks. Thread a tapestry needle with the same yarn from your project, then place your stitches so one half of the live stitches are on a back needle and the other half are on a front needle. You will want the knit side of your project facing you. Enter the first stitch on the front needle as if to purl, using your tapestry needle like a knitting needle. Then enter the first stitch on the back needle as if to knit. Enter the first stitch on the front needle as if to knit, and slide it off. Enter the first stitch on the back needle as if to purl, then slide it off. Enter the next stitch on the front needle as if to purl, and repeat the process: purl in front, knit in back, purl in back and slide off, knit in front and slide off. Repeat until all the stitches have been worked. If you find that your Kitchener stitch is uneven or you are having trouble with tension, a darning egg in the toe of the sock can help. Here is a video guide to Kitchener stitch you may find useful as well: https://www.youtube.com/watch?v=-nlWKvrGp-4.

LONG-TAIL CO

Leaving tail with about 1" (2.5 cm) of yarn for each stitch to be cast-on, make a slipknot in the yarn and place it on the right-hand needle, with the tail to the front and the working end to the back. Insert the thumb and forefinger of your left hand between the strands of yarn so that the working end is around your forefinger and the tail end is around your thumb, "slingshot" fashion; *insert the tip of the right-hand needle into the front loop on the thumb, hook the strand of yarn coming from the forefinger from back to front, and draw it through the loop on your thumb; remove your thumb from the loop and pull on the working yarn to tighten the new stitch on the right-hand needle; return your thumb and forefinger to their original positions and repeat from * for remaining sts to be cast-on. A video may be found here: https://www.youtube.com/watch?v=8wUPQDYtoy0.

MAGIC LOOP

Working in "Magic Loop" means to work on a long circular needle that is arranged in a figure-8 formation in your project. One half of the working stitches for the project remain on the cord of the needle while the other half of working stitches are kept on the needles themselves. Each half is worked and then the cord is drawn up to make room for the next half to be worked. Find a video for this technique here: https://www.youtube.com/watch?v=1mqIqRdJc68.

RUSSIAN JOIN

A Russian Join is created by weaving the ends of two balls of yarn together, with the goal of creating a near-invisible transition from one skein to another in a project. You can find a video online for this technique here: https://www.youtube.com/watch?v=qWrh8VmTJug.

TWO AT A TIME

A variation on the Magic Loop technique, Two at a Time is a method of setting up two similar sleeves, socks, or knit tubes to work them both at the same time, either from individual balls of yarn or from a single, center-pull ball, pulled from both the inside and the outside of the ball. With this method, one half of each tube lives on each "side" of a very long circular needle. You can learn how to set up for TAAT here: https://www.youtube.com/watch?v=lbxZsSpnV5M&t=14s.

guide to resources

ON NATURAL DYEING

Hand Dyed, Anna Joyce (Abrams, 2019)

Journeys in Natural Dyeing, Kristine Vejar and Adrienne Rodriguez (Abrams, 2020)

Make Ink, Jason Logan (Abrams, 2018)

The Modern Natural Dyer, Kristine Vejar (Abrams, 2015)

Dharma Trading Co.
dharmatrading.com

Dyer Supplier
dyersupplier.com

Grand Prismatic Seed
grandprismaticseed.com

ON FIBER

The Knitter's Book of Wool, Clara Parkes (Potter Craft, 2011)

Local Wool podcast, Anastasia Williams
woolanddye.com/podcast

Vanishing Fleece, Clara Parkes (Abrams Press, 2019)

YarnStories podcast, Miriam Felton
yarnstoriespodcast.com

PATTERN YARN RESOURCES

Barrett Wool Co.
barrettwoolco.com/

Beaverslide Dry Goods
beaverslide.com/

Fancy Tiger Crafts
fancytigercrafts.com

Garden Wool & Dye Co.
woolanddye.com

Handspun Hope
handspunhope.org

Harrisville Designs
harrisvilledesigns.com

Hello Yarn
helloyarn.com

Kelbourne Woolens
kelbournewoolens.com

Peace Fleece
peacefleece.com

Retrosaria
retrosaria.rosapomar.com

NOTIONS & TOOLS

Akerworks
akerworks.com

Bookhou
bookhou.com

Churchmouse Yarns & Teas
churchmouseyarns.com

Cocoknits
cocoknits.com

Craft South
craft-south.com

Oritdotan
etsy.com/shop/oritdotan

Plystre
plystre.no

Pom Maker
pommaker.com

TextileGarden
textilegarden.com

acknowledgments

There are so many people without whom this book could have never happened. First and foremost, I need to thank Sue McCain, my exceptional technical editor who walked me through my first major pattern release and some troubling cardigan numbers, and ultimately made sure that everything presented here was knittable. Additionally, I'd like to send my appreciation to the team at Abrams for being eternally patient, encouraging, and understanding throughout the process and throughout what has been one of the busiest years I could have ever imagined!

I would also like to thank my husband, Andrew, and my family for their support and understanding of this massive undertaking. I can never express to you how much I have appreciated having a team of people ready to take on my whining at any moment with relatively little annoyance. I promise that someday I will knit something lovely for each of you, although it may take me a very long time.

To the amazing friends who rallied together to help make this book beautiful: Katie Starks, my immensely talented, kindhearted photographer, who serves as an anchor on every shoot, a gentle but firm cheerleader, and a driving force behind every project we work on together. To Amelia, who helps me manage my own expectations and rallies to every challenge (even being an unexpected model)! To Savannah, whose willingness to help and effervescence shine through in every photo and brighten every moment. To Jess, who lent her comforting presence and exceptional style as my stylist and stunning model. I also want to thank the team of White's Mercantile Room and Board for keeping cool under the pressure of a mistake I made when booking and rose to the occasion to make it all work for me anyway.

I want to extend love to so many people who helped me feel optimistic and passionate about this project throughout its creation: Andrea, Aimee, Veronik, Anastasia, Emily, Tammy, Ellen, Marce, Anne, Teri, Mary Catherine, Sylvia, Bristol, Connie, Julie, Sydney, Jennifer, Marianne, Amanda, and Patricia. Thank you to everyone who has invited me to come to a retreat or to their shop, or suggested me for a workshop—you have helped me achieve my dreams.

I also want to appreciate those who donated or lent yarn, notions, garments, and goods for this book that were not listed in resources: Why Knot Fibers, Hickory Hollow Soap, Salt River Mills Yarn, Stonehedge Fiber Mill, Cestar Sheep & Wool Company, and Elizabeth Suzann. Thank you to the knitting community for expanding the scope of my goals to make this a worthy addition to your homes and studios.

about the author

Hannah Thiessen has had a lifelong relationship with texture, color, and language. The daughter of an artist and writer, she grew up throughout the American South, living in Georgia, Kentucky, and Virginia, and then moving to Iowa during her senior year. She lives in the greater Nashville area with her husband, Andrew, and cats Leopold and Thusa. Hannah dreams of someday leaving the city and moving to the country where she can dive deep into homesteading and fiber culture, but for now, she explores weaving, spinning, painting, quilting, writing, and sewing from her cozy suburban home.

Hannah travels for her work as the production editor of *By Hand* serial and can also be found teaching workshops around the country. She shares her pursuits on her website, hannahthiessen.com, and on Instagram as @hannahbelleknits.